A Walk in My Shoes

OUR LIVES OF HOPE

An Oral History of the Artists of the
"Made in Honduras Craft Co-op"
TRUJILLO, HONDURAS

DIANE KARPER

Alan C. Hood & Company, Inc.
CHAMBERSBURG, PENNSYLVANIA

A Walk in My Shoes

ISBN: 978-0-911469-35-6

Library of Congress Cataloging-in-Publication Data

Karper, Diane, 1949-
 A walk in my shoes : our lives of hope : an oral history of the artists of
the "Made in Honduras Craft Co-op," Trujillo, Honduras / Diane Karper.
    p. cm.
 ISBN 978-0-911469-35-6 (pbk.)
 1. Artisans--Honduras--Biography. 2. Artists--Honduras--Biography. 3.
Handicraft--Honduras--Trujillo. 4. Decorative arts--Honduras--Trujillo. 5.
Cooperative societies--Honduras--Trujillo. 6. Oral history--Honduras. 7.
Hope--Case studies. 8. Spiritual biography--Honduras. 9.
Honduras--Biography. 10. Honduras--Rural conditions. I. Title.
 TT31.H8K37 2010
 745.092'2--dc22

                          2010013431

                 Published by Alan C. Hood & Co., Inc.
                 Chambersburg, Pennsylvania 17201

           10 9 8 7 6 5 4 3 2 1

A Walk in My Shoes

OUR LIVES OF HOPE

And this is love:
that we walk in obedience to his commands.
As you have heard from the beginning,
his command is that you walk in love.

2 JOHN 6

Table of Contents

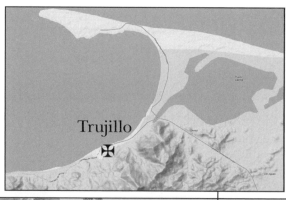

Trujillo

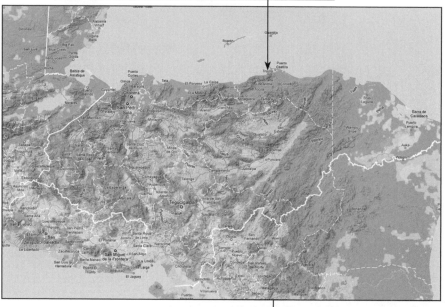

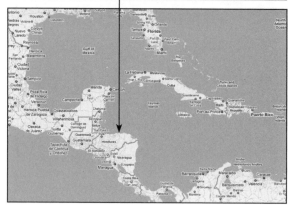

Introduction

Scott and Diane Karper with Queen

If someone could walk in your shoes, what would they see? What would they feel? What would they know about you? Even for a day, the glimpses of your life would change how that person thinks about you. You would have become more real, more personal to them.

Scott and I have been living and working in Honduras for eleven years with Christian Veterinary Mission. We walk with the people, responding to their needs, helping them make decisions that can change their lives, and showing them Christ's love through the work that we do. We love being here. We love helping so many friends in the walk. While Scott is teaching the farmers how to better care for their animals, I have been working with their wives, helping them develop skills that can be marketed to put food on their tables. Over the years, this has grown into a craft co-op of about sixty people. They have a beautiful store in Trujillo where they sell their goods. They also have a website that you will want to visit: www.hondurastreasures. com (and you can also see all the photos from this book in color on this site.) This project has changed many lives, given hope to the hopeless, and introduced Christian principles in their daily walks. Self-esteem has risen. This confident group of artists is ready to share their stories with you so that they become more real and more personal to you.

That is the purpose of this book: To let you walk in the shoes of a few people who wanted to share their stories with you. They have opened their hearts and lives to you so that you might know them and their walk in this world. I know this will forever change the way you view them and their friends who live here in Honduras.

Many tears were shed over these stories…in real life and then in the telling. Many times I stopped and told the writer that we didn't have to do this. Always I got the same response, " Diane, you are the first person who ever cared enough to ask. I need to tell my story." To imagine my friends in some of the situations described in their stories was emotionally draining. I had to stop between each telling to be prepared for the next one, but never was prepared to hear what was told to me. I thought I knew these folks…they had been my dear friends for years. Together we had walked on muddy paths, cried over mistakes, studied Bible stories, jumped over raging creeks, struggled over new products and quality control, prayed over friends who were killed or dying, rejoiced over new births, swam in the ocean, traveled to far off cities looking for markets, experienced elevators, escalators, and crowded buses, eaten tamales, and sang songs. But I never knew what got them to the place where we had met. I had thought I could compile these stories in a few months; instead it has been two years. Many of the writers came to me separately asking if I had forgotten to get their story. It was their drive that kept me going. It is their desire to share their lives with you.

Of course we can't walk in somebody else's shoes, nor change what has happened in the past. But because these few people are willing to share their experiences with you, it can change the future. It can change how you view them and others like them in the world. It is a small step in making the world a better place.

Each one should use whatever gifts he has received
to serve others, faithfully administering
God's grace in its various forms.

1 PETER 4:10

Ale's Story

Ale with his puzzle

I am Alexis Chacon, but most people call me Ale. I was born in May of 1984 in Masapa on a coffee finca* where my father and mother worked. I am the oldest male of twelve brothers and sisters. We grew up close to one another in a one-room mud and straw hut with a tin roof. The room was divided with sacks to make a small kitchen area in the daytime. We slept on patate mats on the floor and on frame beds of twine. If you were one of the fortunate ones you got a hammock. Food was scarce, but we seldom complained…it was just the way of life, and we didn't know anything different. My father worked at the big hacienda† for about ten years, then we moved to San Augustine, Yoro, to a smaller finca that he bought for his own. It was a beautiful place high in the Honduran mountains where it is always cool, but our housing situation was the same. My father raised beans and corn, and chopped pastures for other campesinos‡. My father taught me how to work for a living.

When I was six years old I was playing by a pond and fell in. I couldn't swim, but my older sister was nearby and threw a stick for me to grab onto. She pulled me in to safety. I know God was watching over me.

Another accident occurred when I was thirteen years old. I was traveling down the mountain in a pick-up truck with other folks from our village. The brakes gave way and the truck tumbled over a cliff, rolling onto its side and trapping my leg. They eventually got me free and took me to San Pedro Sula in great pain. My leg was not just broken, but smashed. Doctors pulled and pushed the bones back into place… again I was in great pain since they did not give me any anesthesia. (This is something you have to buy here…anesthesia, and we didn't have any money). Then they hung my leg on a hook above the bed to keep it in position…for days. It was very uncomfortable. My mother sat with me the whole time, as nurses in the hospital are few, and care for the patient is the responsibility of family members. But again, God watched over

*finca: a small farm. †hacienda: a farmhouse. ‡campesino: a peasant farmer.

me, and I healed enough to be sent home. It was months until I could walk again.

My parents think education is important, so they sent me to school when we moved to Yoro and I was ten. I graduated from sixth grade at seventeen. Immediately I began a relationship with Maria Ramirez. She lived in the same village as my family, and seemed like a nice girl. Her father and mother kept her at the house all the time, so we seldom crossed paths. But when we did, she caught my eye. She was a hard worker, getting up early to do her chores. She was responsible for making food for the workers at her father's finca, so I knew she would be a good woman in my house. Plus she is pretty and has little dimples when she smiles.

Ale, Maria, and family

We decided to move to my parents' house together. We lived there for eight days while I built a small hut of mud and sticks for us. In this time Maria was pregnant with our first son, Samuel. He was born at home in our little hut. It was scary for me to think I was now responsible for a new little life. He was so precious, and I loved holding him and giving him his bottle. But to put milk in the bottle was a problem, since I didn't have any work that paid regularly. After doing many day jobs for a year, Maria and I decided to try our luck at looking for work off the mountain. We had relatives who went to Trujillo and got jobs. So we thought we should try this too. We saved money (Maria is very good at this, I am not) for the bus fare, and left home with Samuel and a backpack filled with his powdered milk, bottle, a blanket, a few dresses for Maria, and a set of clothes for me. We had hopes of getting work and a job right away.

It didn't happen. I tried my hand at a local supermarket for a month...but they laid me off after the first pay (thirty dollars). Then I got a job loading cement blocks on a truck. That was about two dollars per day....and only a day here and there. I also started making blocks with family members, but it was temporary. I finally got into making charcoal...a very dirty business. You have to dig a pit, collect the wood that is the right size, cut it into sticks that fit into your hole in the ground, layer them and leaves and grass in the pit, cover it all and light it, leaving it to simmer for days. After it was cooked just right, you bagged it and rode all over creation looking for a place that wanted to buy it. When they bought it, you had enough money in your hand

Ale working

to buy Samuel milk for a couple of days. Maria was unhappy and wanted to return...but we had no money for the bus fare back. We were living with my aunt and her family, but they didn't share their food...and any food I found they expected us to share with them too. I tried to help out at their house by looking for firewood for them...after I worked, or looked for work all day. It was difficult. So we moved to the house of another aunt and her family. They were a little better as they shared their food with us and we shared our food with them, when we could get any to share. I went fishing with my uncle who tried teaching me the trade. Maria helped them to sew clothes for their girls. Again, I helped with the firewood. And kept looking for work.

The neighbor's watchman told us we could move into a cement block, no-roof, rotting, one-room house on some land across the road. The owner lived in Italy and said we could be there until she came. So we searched for tin scraps, and found a few old pieces that we put on top of the blocks and held it there with rocks. We added a door with a lock. We built a mud stove for cooking, and slept on the floor. Home Sweet Home! I was still searching for a permanent, paying job....just as most Hondurans are hoping for.

As fate would have it, I found two jobs at the same time. Some gringos* lived across the road and were being robbed all the time, so they asked me to be their watchman whenever they would leave the house. I took the job. And then, that same day I heard from a guy who wanted me to be his cement block maker for his two houses he was building. It was five miles

*gringo: a foreigner, not a derogatory term in Honduras

away, but the gringo said I could borrow his bike to get there at 4:00 AM every morning, and Maria could sit at their house whenever they left.

Block-making was grueling work in the heat of the day, so it was best to start early. I usually made about thirty blocks per day, and got paid ten cents per block. I would finish around 3:00 PM and ride my bike back home. Then I would hopefully get to eat something…and then go off looking for firewood so Maria could cook me food for the next day. Many days there was nothing to eat, and no money to buy anything. Working was so hard then. It was a tiring life, but was work. Maria watched the gringo's house for me when they needed to leave while I was working. They paid us cash every two weeks. Life was looking up. With this money we were even getting food most days. And I liked living in Trujillo with the mountains meeting the sea. At the end of a long hot day, I could swim in the ocean if I had time to relax.

Since Maria was sitting at the gringos' house, she was learning things

Ale cutting a guacal for a drum

from them. She learned how to paint rocks into little houses that tourists bought. Can you believe that she sold enough of them to buy a gas stove so that I wouldn't have to go out looking for firewood at the end of a long day? Our parents are still laughing at us buying a stove with rocks. But this definitely freed up time for me to enjoy life more.

In 2004, I was riding my bike in the rain looking for milk for Samuel. A pick up truck came up behind me and hit me, knocking me over the truck and slamming my head as I fell. The owner threw me into the back of his truck and took me to the hospital in Trujillo. I was unconscious for weeks, so was just told about these things. Trujillo took x-rays, and threw me on a gurney that Maria had to push through the halls...and she didn't know how to drive it, or open the doors...and the nurses wouldn't help her. After four hours of nothing, doctors decided I had to go to San Pedro Sula to the hospital there, seven hours away. They loaded me on the ambulance that the gringos paid for. As it turns out, the ambulance is just an empty van with a red light on it! My brother-in-law rode with me, since they wouldn't let Maria go along. Seems you had to be able to lift the patient in and out yourself! Maria came over on a bus. The gringos kept Samuel while she was gone. Maria sat outside my room while the doctors didn't do anything, since she was not allowed inside. Yes, after the long ride, we arrived in San Pedro Sula when there was some massive accident that had the entire hospital tied up with emergencies. So I waited another twelve hours to be seen. To me, it didn't matter, I was unconscious. Maria said I did wake up once and wanted to go to the bathroom. She called a nurse to come help me, but nobody was free.... meantime I had decided to get up...and immediately fell at the foot of the bed. I laid there crumpled in a ball for the rest of the night until someone finally came in to get me in the morning. Care is not good in the hospitals in Honduras. They make you wait for hours to be seen, and if you haven't died by then, they will look at you, and maybe treat you. I was in the hospital for a month, then I went to my parents' house to be cared for. I finally woke up...but didn't know who anyone was, nor remember anything about life. My family took me to a healer, and massage person. My collar bone was broken, and the hospital had not set it, so this guy did...painfully. Then we got back in the truck for the ride back up the mountain. It is a bumpy ride to say the least...and the collar bone popped out of place again. So back we went the next day. Through all of this, Maria nursed me to health. It was two months when I returned to Trujillo, on pain killers, and not walking nor thinking well. But with the help of friends and family, I have completely recovered and am living life to the fullest again. God once again protected me.

The gringo, Scott, and I became good friends. He taught me how to make things from wood. He first showed me how to make folding chairs. I tried to sell them for Semana Santa...but nobody bought anything. Then he showed me how to make a table for my house. And he taught me how to make wooden puzzles to sell to their workteams. I was amazed at how the teams would come through and buy everything. They loved my puzzles. Then Scott showed me how to make thumb drums from calabash. Those are my biggest seller. I also make necklaces and earrings from calabash. Scott showed me how to carve the tree of life into them with a tiny hand saw blade. People really like them too. Scott is always thinking up new ideas for me to try...he is so creative. I am making nativity set puzzles too. It is fun working with him, and great making money for doing these fun things. I have had a few bad cuts on the table saw. One really chewed up my thumb...I am lucky to have one still.

Diane is Scott's wife and has taught Maria to make many things too: rock painting, hats, visors, book covers, Bible covers, painted shirts, cards, shell earrings, and sea glass jewelry. Together we could open a small craft store with these new found skills.

We are members of a craft co-operative, Made In Honduras. We each make our crafts, about sixty of us. And we have built our own store where we all work a couple days per month to run it. I am the watchman for the store, Maria is the manager. Our family lives in the apartment below the store for free (payment for our work). It is so nice to have a cement home with two bedrooms, a living room and kitchen and indoor bathroom. I helped with the construction everyday for six months, so learned a lot about building. I am now almost finished building an adobe house for our family to live in Yoro someday.

Our second son, Ariel, was born in Sept 2006. He is a delight to my heart, just as Samuel is. Our lives have changed dramatically since I started making money in the crafts and as watchman for the gringos. (I no longer am their watchman because they moved to another house.) Maria and I have bought a few cows, and a couple

Ale, Maria, and sons on family trip

of manzanas* of a coffee finca up in the mountains by our parents. One day we will move to our house up there. For now, we go up for the coffee harvest, and to visit family when we can. I am the most successful of the kids in the family, so I have helped my father build my mother a new cement house with a cement floor and tile roof. She is so happy to have a big house and not to be living in cramped quarters like she was for all of her life.

Maria and I have had our ups and down. Like the time that a young, pretty girl in the neighborhood decided she liked me. The girl would walk past the house all the time, or look me up on the beach. Maria wasn't happy about this...and ran off to her parents. Her father sent her back and told her to work things out. We did. Then I ran off once too...just too much responsibility and no answers. But I realized my life was better with Maria than without her. She ran off once more, leaving me scared that I would not get to live with my sons and her. But she is back permanently now. I think we have both matured and will be together for this lifetime. I want to get married...but Maria has been afraid to go this route. I think God would be happy if we did. She is pregnant with our third child now...a girl. We are so excited. God is so good to us.

Ale's family on the beach

manzana: a measure of land area; approximately 1.75 acre

Amparo's Story

Amparo with her bags

I am Maria Amparo Amaya. Call me by my middle name, like my friends and family do. On October 30, 1964, I was born into a then small family in San Marcos, Colomancagua in the department of Intubuca in the western mountains of Honduras. My father had three children to another woman who had died. I was his first child to my mother. Eventually I had five other brothers and sisters to share our small, one-room, mud floor, adobe house with a tile roof. It was a large enough room to divide it with coffee sacks to make more private rooms for all of us for sleeping, sitting, and cooking.

I had chores to do. My sister and I had to carry the family's drinking and cooking water three times per day...six trips each time. We balanced a big clay pot on our heads and walked with it three kilometers to the house. This was heavy work for little girls, but it was expected of us, and we never knew anything else. I also helped with the wash on Saturdays. This was done in a river about four kilometers from the house. I loved it when I got to go with my mother to do the wash. After we finished washing the clothes, we laid them over rocks to dry. While they were drying, my mother would talk to other women and I could go play in the water, looking for chacalines (crayfish). Sometimes we found huge ones...what a feast when we got home!

My father had many small jobs. His main job was making guara* from sugar cane. He made juice and candies to cover his trade. But his money came from the guara he made at a secret place up in the mountains. He never got caught when the soldiers came looking for the

*guara: sugarcane liquor

illegal brewers because his place was well hidden in the mountain. He also was a merchant who bought and sold animals, grain…anything you wanted to buy or sell. He taught me well about business. I often walked with him on his buying and selling trips. He also took me to celebrations at people's houses where I led the dancing for the party. We got paid in food. I felt very special being with my Papi.

Papi sent me to school through fourth grade. That is as many grades as our little community school had. When I was twelve years old, we left and moved to Buenos Aires, near Florida de Copan. My oldest sister had a coffee finca there, so we went to work on her finca for a few years. With the money we made there, my father bought a small coffee finca of his own. I helped harvest the coffee. When I was fifteen, I became the cook for my family of eleven plus all the workers on our finca. Daily, I ground the corn to make tortillas. I cooked eggs, rice, beans, and made cheese for the group. Lots of the workers were interested in me, but my father made it clear that they could have a job, but not me. But they gave me lots of attention, since I was very pretty. I remember praying to God that He should help me choose the right one by putting him in my path.

I was thirteen when I met Medardo. He too had moved to our village from Intibuca. He was working on another coffee finca. We were friends for two years, talking and walking together. He was always in my path.

Amparo sewing at home

My father did not like Medardo, who was six years older than me. When I was fifteen, we tried to run off together...three times. Each time we got caught...and I got beat. Papi loved me, but could be very hard. He used a belt or a rope to let me know I was not doing what he wanted. So when I was sixteen years old, Medardo and I decided to get married in the church. That way, Papi...nor anyone else could divide us. This seemed to appease Papi. He came to the wedding without any objections. I said my vows before my family, my husband, and God. I believe what I said, and live by that still...even though Medardo has had some indiscretions.

At seventeen, our first child was born, Irma. We moved to Rio Chiquita, near Bonita Oriental in Colon. Medardo got work there cutting wood for lumber. He worked on contract, cutting the trees with an ax and then slicing the lumber with a hand saw. It was hard, tiring work. Every weekend Madardo drank his pay away with his buddies. He got drunk, stumbled home where I put him to bed. He was never aggressive or nasty when he was drunk. It was just such a waste of our precious little money. I often asked him to please stop. But he couldn't...or wouldn't. We had a total of five kids at that time. It was incredible to me. One day when he was drunk, our oldest son, who was six at the time, asked him why he was doing it. And why he was wasting our money, when we didn't have money

Amparo helping with homework

to waste. Medardo came home and asked me if I had put our son up to this. I hadn't. Medardo stopped his weekend drinking, realizing how it was affecting our kids and me. Once in a while he would still go with his friends and get drunk. But even that stopped. Now, he never drinks. We had more kids…fourteen to be exact.

Medardo stopped cutting trees when it became more difficult to get permits to cut. He started making doors and tables for people in his carpenter shop. He also went out to chop grass and pastures for others.

I stayed home with the kids, taking care of the house, cooking, washing, cleaning. I also went back to school finishing sixth grade. I learned to do business with my father, so I had a mind for figures. I would take any money we had and go to the lottery and buy tickets to double our money. This worked sometimes…I still do this. I buy for myself and others, making a little money on the side.

In 2000, I heard on the radio that there was a land invasion not too far away near Trujillo. The people had moved onto some land that the Honduran government set aside for poor peasants to claim for their own. This seemed interesting to me because we had no land of our own, and this was maybe a way of securing a future for our family. I talked to Medardo about it, but he said we would get killed…he had heard about the troubles

Amparo with sewing group

this group had when they arrived. Many people were killed by rich land owners of the area who didn't want the peasants to have the land...even though the Honduran government had put it aside for the poor to claim if they wanted it. I went to meet with the coordinator of this group in the village they were calling Guadalupe Carney, named for a priest who was martyred in land reformation in the 1980's. He invited us to join them if we paid an entrance fee, and vowed to stand by the group in their fight for the land. After talking this over, Medardo and I decided it was worth the risk to maybe get some land and future for our kids. I have been a village leader over these past ten years. I also went to a sewing class and learned to sew. I joined nine other women from the village and started a sewing group. We joined a craft group, Made In Honduras, to sell the bags and dresses that we make. We are now also painting silk scarves.

When we were married twenty-five years, Medardo and I had our first big problems. I got pregnant and he began running around with other women. My pregnancy made him mad...he didn't want MORE responsibility. I cried all the time. I yelled at him when he did come home. I never slept. I found out who the young girl was that he was seeing, and called her parents. We met...all of us. Medardo and the girl never admitted to anything. The parents sent her off to San Pedro Sula so she wouldn't be near Medardo...but she still calls him. I am suffering. But I refuse to give in to his immaturity. I went to a naturalist (witch), who said that Medardo was under a spell. She told me that Medardo could not love me while he was under the spell. For L.6000*, she could cast an alternative spell and get him back for me. I never have been able to come up with the money, so can't get the spell released. Friends tell me this is not something to believe...but what else can I do? I had always felt life was good until this problem came up.

I have always believed in many superstitions of my people. Some are just crazy...but others are true. Like if you want to know if your unborn child is male or female, you wrap a spoon in a towel, and a fork in another. Give them to a friend to put on the ground. Then have your friend invite you to sit on one of them. If you sit on the spoon, you will have a girl...the fork is a boy. You must repeat this three times to get the correct response...if it is the same all three times your answer is correct. It worked for my daughter's birth. But for my last son, I never got the spoon or fork all three times, so I never knew.

*L. or lempira: Honduran currency; about twenty equals one U. S. dollar

I work hard to find jobs for my family. I push my children to be hard workers, so that they might get ahead in life. I saved money to send our oldest son North. He had been there for years, illegally, sending us money for the family to eat, and to build him a house for his return. People in the US are mad at Hondurans for coming and taking jobs. My son was cutting grass along the side of the roads...is there anyone of you who wants to do this job? The illegals who have gone with him are working picking fruit and vegetables. Is there anyone of you who wants this job? Others are working cleaning streets with a broom. Is there anyone of you who wants this job? It is MONEY for us. It is a hundred times the money he could make here. So why are you mad? He was paying his taxes, and doing the work you do not want to do...and sending us money to live. He loves your country. He says it is clean and beautiful. But he loves Honduras more. He returned here once his house was built. Of course, now he has a woman and son, and house, but no money.

Money...always a problem. Those of us who don't have it, want it...and think it will cure everything. (We think we could use it better than we see the rich folks using their money.) I wonder if I will ever get a chance to know if that is true.....

Amparo, Medardo and family

Chave's Story

Chave with her products

I am Maria Isabel Paz...but everyone calls me Chave. I don't know why. I was born on March 3rd, 1984...the last child in our family, so I got lots of attention from my mother and father and siblings. We lived in a mud hut with a thatch roof in the mountains above Morazon in Yoro. I have six brothers and sisters, and another four from my father's first family. We all slept on patates (mats) on the floor. My oldest sister, Tonia was my babysitter. We all played daily pretending to cook food and coffee from mud. In real life we ate rice, beans, eggs, and tortillas for our daily meals. We seldom had any meat that I can remember. When I was five I had to start doing chores with the others. My job was to haul water from the creek about a mile away, but because I was the youngest, I didn't have to do many other things.

My father was a hunter...but sold most of his meat for money to buy the staples for us. He would go to the mountains daily hunting with his dogs. And he would often bring me a stick of sugar cane when he returned. Only for me, not the others. He would also plant corn and beans for other people. All of us helped with the harvest. We could get L.20 per day if we worked from 7:00 AM to 7:00 PM...that is one dollar. When I was older I helped to harvest coffee too. For this we got paid L.8 per gallon. All the money went to the family for food and clothes.

I went to school for three years. Then my father died. This was the saddest day of my life. We tried to keep him comfortable, but it was horrible to watch him suffer. He was in pain and couldn't breathe. I will never forget how helpless I felt. At eight I couldn't imagine how life could go on without my father to care for us. And things did change: We didn't have any money for buying the books, uniforms, and paying tuition at school, so I had to quit and work the fields with the family. I loved school…especially Dia del Nino* when all the kids got special food and we had a piñata. In my house we never had any toys to

Chave's workshop at home

play with. I never had a new dress, or new shoes, or new backpack. Being the last child, I got all hand-me-downs. My mother sewed my dresses from rags, and made me bags to carry for a backpack. Now, without my father, things were even harder to come by.

When I was twelve, I started dating Herman. I knew him all my life since he lived in the same village as we did, and he cut coffee in the same finca that we worked in. Actually, my older sister lived with his older brother. Our dates consisted of him coming to my house. He was fifteen. At fourteen, I moved in with him. So did my mother since she

was alone now. But Herman had no work, so we all decided to move to Trujillo, where our other family members had gone and found work. Herman began a job making blocks, which he still is doing today. Making blocks is hard work, since here we make them one block at a time. First you need to mix the cement by hand, to the right consistency. Then you fill the block mold and pound it firm so that when you take the mold off, the block can stand in the sun to dry. And you start a new block. But you have to make sure the sun

Chave with her bags

Dia del Nino: A holiday in Honduras, "Day of the Child"

Chave's old house

Chave's new house

isn't drying the blocks too fast, so you need to wet them down. Herman can make about 150 blocks per day. He is exhausted at the end of a day. He is building us a new house of cement. I am paying for it with my money from selling my jewelry in the co-op. We have the roof on, but no windows or doors yet. But we are living in it since we have no other place to go. We were living in a shack on the beach as watchmen, but the new owners accused me of stealing their chickens, so we moved out. I would never steal anybody's anything, let alone their chickens!

There was another very sad day in my life when my brother was killed while riding his bike. He was hit by a car that was driven by a guy high on marijuana. He left a wife and two little girls. He was always such a happy person and loved his family so much.

When we moved to Trujillo, we got a job as watchmen on a property at the beach, thinking it would help pay the bills. But the landlord seldom paid us. The house was free, but tumbling down, and often flooded in the rains. While we were living in this shack, I was looking for ways to make us some money. Jobs are few and far between in Trujillo...it is not the rich job market that rumors led us to believe. But one day I noticed my sister,

Chave's dinner

Tonia, making some mirrors lined with shells. She said she was selling them with a craft group that was just starting. I wanted to join this group. But I had no skills and didn't know how to get in. I asked the gringa organizer, Diane, to help me learn some craft to make for the group. She showed me how to make some simple necklaces and earrings from beads and magnets. This might sound simple to you, but to me it was a life changing

Chave working with Fredi

project. I felt creative for the first time in my life. And I was making things that other people wanted to buy. I was making money. Diane insisted that I remember to put half of my earnings away for buying more materials. But I always had so many bills and necessities that I never could manage that. Last year, Diane returned from a trip with a beautiful cell phone bag of velvet with beaded designs on it. I loved it and decided to learn how to make this bag. It was hard at first, but now I am making them so well. And people are buying them as fast as I can make them. I also make little people pins and statues from beads. And I make braided bracelets and earrings. I love my work and the money it brings to help me feed the family…I have three sons and am pregnant with our fourth child now.

My hopes for the future are to finish our new house, and to have my three boys finish sixth grade (and more if they can). I know God is watching out for my family. He has given me more opportunities than I ever would have believed possible. I look forward to the future.

Chave, Herman, and their sons

Ena's Story

Ena and her embroidery

My name is Ena Pradi Inestroza Fuentes. I was born in 1978 in Suyapita Guayape, in Orlancho. I have six brothers and five sisters. We were one beautiful family. We went to church everyday and every Sunday. My Papi raised beans and corn. Every time he sold his beans, he would buy each of us new pants or dress and shoes. Every Sunday we wore the same new clothes to church, until he sold beans again next year.

One year gringos from Germany came to our town to open a day care center. I now understand that they took our photos to send to friends who would send money to support each of us in the center. But at the time I was scared to death because they took my photo. I had no idea what a camera was, nor how I got onto that piece of paper. I cried for a long time and was very afraid of those gringos. Eventually the center opened and my parents took all of us kids there while they went off to work in the fields. It was a wonderful place to spend your childhood, with balls and swings. They had classes that taught us how to embroider and sew. I loved doing this hand work (and still love it today). There were thirty-eight kids and five teachers in the center that we attended from 7:00 in the morning until four in the afternoon. We would play ball, build houses from cardboard boxes, and do crafts. For me, the center was my home. I loved it.

When I was eight years old, I began to go to the school in the village because the sponsors paid for that. I was a very good student, and was also on the folk dance team. We would sing and dance in various places in the community all the years I was in the school. We even went to one big competition in Juticalpa. We walked 1 hour everyday to the school, and one hour home again. We loved school. For 15th of September (our Independence Day) I was part of a special dance team with a good dance partner. We practiced for weeks. It was going to be a wonderful presentation. But at this same time, my father left my mother for another woman. He said I had to quit the dance team, and couldn't do our presentation for 15th of September. I was devastated. He would not talk to me nor help me. He never visited us again, and didn't want us to visit him. My happy life was coming to an end. The other kids in the school teased both my sister and me. And at this same time, the Germans closed the day care center. We lost all of our assistance. I could no longer go on to school. Life looked bleak: no songs, no dance, no crafts, no school, no sponsors, no money to get new clothes, no regular food.

My mother took us to live with my grandmother and aunts in the mountain while she went off to Tegucigalpa to look for a job. She began working as the cook/housecleaner for a rich family in Teguc*. Every six months she would come home for a few days, bringing us clothes and candy. I remembered my old life well, but couldn't get it back again. I didn't like living in the cramped one-room, and sleeping on a cot that had to be folded up everyday. I had a pretty blue bottle that I found in our school one day. I kept that blue bottle with me for years, sleeping with it and carrying it everywhere. It reminded me of the beautiful life I once had. My new life was all work. We washed clothes every Saturday. Every other day of the week we walked in the mountains looking for fire wood. We never relaxed.

Ena's home work space

Teguc: slang for Tegucigalpa

Ena with her product at the craft store

When I was twelve, I left home with David, a friend who was sixteen and nice to me. We went to the mountain called Piedra Negra to cut mahogany. We stayed there for a month, then for two months we planted beans and corn for his family and us. I turned thirteen and was pregnant with our first child. David's family was the family I didn't have. They were moving to Trujillo to look for work, so we went with them. David was trained as a construction worker and welder. There was no work for him in the mountains, but we heard that Trujillo was growing and might have work. Every couple of years I had another baby. My job was to stay home and care for them and the house and cook meals for everyone. I spent all my days cooking, cleaning, and doing the wash. I never had anything else to do. We lived in a cane house with a thatched roof over by the lagoon. We built our place on some land where other folks had decided to build too. None of us had any way of buying land, and nobody wanted the land by the lagoon because of all the bugs. So we lived there.

Until Hurricane Mitch moved us! The rains and wind were terrible. The house fell. Then the water rose and swept away everything we owned. We trudged though water to get to the safety of the grade school. A man in a truck was out looking for people to help them get to safety at the school. We stayed there eight days with hundreds of other folks. Some had brought food, so we all shared it. We all slept on the floor, and worried over what we were to do next. When the storm subsided, we went back to find nothing. David had lots of work to do though, so we did manage a little better than some folks. With his money from working, we had milk and then a stove, and then could make tortillas and rice. We set up a cane and mud house again.

Five years later, we got a job as watchmen on a property by the beach. The landowners don't pay us, but they give us a place to live, and we guard their property. They rented out their house to some development workers from the agriculture school at Zamorano. The girl who was renting showed me how to make beads from bamboo that was growing on the property. I showed my sister-in-law how to do this, and we made a few necklaces. Together we decided to go to the gringa, Diane, we had seen working with other folks from the area. We hoped she would buy our necklaces. I was afraid to go alone, since I didn't know this person, and wasn't sure that bamboo was really something that would sell. We nervously walked a mile down the road to her house to talk to her. She thought our ideas were good, and gave us some colorful beads to string between our bamboo. She showed us how to tie knots well, and to make our product perfect. Then she invited us to sell our things with the group that was just forming. We were shocked…and excited at this possibility. But what was more amazing to us was the sale. We went to the gringa's house to set up for a workteam that was going to come to buy souvenirs. Diane is very particular on how things are to be displayed. It looked great… and then the team came. Those ten Americans went through there like army ants, piling necklaces, bags, dolls, and drums into their hands. We couldn't imagine anyone with

Ena with her kids

enough money to pay for all of these things. But they did. And it was the beginning of a new life for me. I still make bamboo necklaces, but have moved on to making beautiful embroidered tablecloths and dresses, and crocheted wire and stone jewelry. It is a wonderful existence again. Our group has built our own store, where each of us works two days a month to keep it open. We receive all the money from our sales, and are in charge of our lives. We have a hope for the future. We are able to feed our children, and send them to school. We are even saving some money to build a cement house.

I am fortunate to have a loving man, four healthy children, some skills that God helped me get when I was young, and now a place to use them. I no longer sit on my steps doing nothing. I am busy all the time with life doing things that I love.

Ena, David, and family

Gladis's Story

Gladis with her recycled paper bead necklaces

My name is Gladis Antonia Ramirez Romero. I am the only one in our family that goes by Romero which is my grandmother's name, not my mother's as is the custom here. I don't know when I was born since nobody ever celebrated my birthday or my life. I am so amazed that anyone would even ask me to tell my story, but have always wanted to tell someone that I am here. I was born in El Negrito, which is a small mountain village in Yoro. My identity card says I was born on August 10, 1977...but these cards are often wrong. I am the oldest of nine children. I remember nothing of my childhood but work and punishment. We lived in a two-room mud hut with a tin roof . My father had many jobs, but mainly planted beans and corn for others. Eventually he got land of his own and planted coffee. But from the time I was three or so, I had to make tortillas for everyone. I got punished with belts, hands, ropes, and pans for not making the tortillas right. I also had to grind the corn and eventually the coffee for my father. When they added more kids to the family, I was in charge of watching them, especially Maria, since she was the only other girl at the time. If anyone got hurt, I got punished. My mother taught me to wash and to cook so she could go out and run errands. She was very good at dishing out harsh punishments, beating me regularly. One day she hit me with a frying pan on the head and chopped it down on my wrist, breaking my wrist. And I was still expected to make tortillas, which of course was impossible. But as terrible as the punishments were from my mother, my father's were worse. He would use his belt too, but preferred a big thick rope that he would whack me with. One day he was so mad at me for something I can't even remember, that he picked me up and shook me hard, breaking both of my arms. I was in such pain. My

*Vivian and cousin
holding the beads*

grandmother came and found me and took me away for a few years, telling my parents they couldn't raise me.

At my grandmother's house, I didn't get hit, but I still worked. She sent me to school for the first time, but I was so slow at learning that the teachers advised her to take me out. I had learned to write my name. That is all. I am embarrassed to say I can't read or write anything. While at my grandmother's house I met Dario. He was nice to be around and we liked each other lots. My mother heard about this and got really mad, saying I had to come home. My grandmother went and got me an ID card and put her name on it (which is why I have her name and not my mother's). But that didn't stop my parents from dragging me back to their house. Dario came for me and we ran off together to his parents' home in Orlanchito when I was sixteen. I was very nervous and scared that my parents would find us and beat me again. I cried lots because I was so scared. Dario's parents didn't like me because I was so sad all the time. He got a job near Sava and we moved into a small house that we still rent today. It is a one-room cement and slab wood house with a mud floor. We have crammed a couple of beds and a table into it, but mostly we live outside. We have no television, plumbing, or electricity at the house. I raise pigs for food for the family. My husband works in the banana fields, so we always have bananas to fill our bellies.

Dario and I had four children together. The second one was killed when he was six years old. I feel terrible and cry about this still. Because I was punished so hard as a child, I decided never to do that to my own children. So my own children often don't listen because they know I won't hit them. One day we were walking on the busy road when my 6-year old was jumping all around and acting crazy. I grabbed his hand and pulled him along with me to keep him at my side. He pulled free of my hand with such force that he fell backwards into the path of a passing pickup truck. He was killed instantly. I will never forgive myself for this accident. If only I hadn't grabbed his hand...If only I could relive this day and have a better outcome. As it is, I pass his grave every time I walk to our house from the main road. And I pass the spot where he died every time I enter the path to our house. You would think I could stop crying over his death, but I have not. I thought having another baby would help me. Vivian is a precious little girl, but she doesn't bring back the brother she never knew.

From an early age, I had learned to start each day talking to God, asking Him to protect me and help me with my work for the day. I continue to do this.

I think because I cared for Maria when she was young, she now cares for me. She helps me with food and money when I need it. She has a good job working in a craft group. And she has a nice house that we can visit, where there is electricity and a television and running water and food. She gives us a cushion to sleep on and cares for us. I love visiting her...I am happiest when I am at her house. Maria wanted me to try to get into this craft group and she and Diane gave me some ideas to try to make. I have tried and tried, but only recently came up with a product that seems to be selling. I sewed quilts, made nativities, necklaces, earrings....nothing sold well. But now I am making paper beads from recycled newspapers. They are very pretty and amazingly are selling fast. A woman on one of the Bay Islands opened a store to sell recycled products at the same time that I began the beads. God really does watch over us. These beads are giving me a hope for the future that I couldn't have otherwise. I joined the crafts group and work in the store two days per month. Maria is always there to help me since I can't write anything well. I have a dream to save enough money to buy a small piece of property and build our own house someday. I live with the constant reminder of the life I have lived. My hand and arms pain me terribly all the time. My son's grave is a reminder of what could have been. But now I have something to work for and a way to reach that goal. This craft project has given me a new identity and a new life.

Gladis with Mel and Vivian

Hilda's Story

Hilda and her dolls

I am Hilda Mejia Pinera. On December 13, 1979, I was born in El Carmen, Morazon, Yoro, where my father was a grass cutter. He also cleared land for coffee farms. I lived my first nine years in El Carmen in a very isolated, mud house with a slab wood roof. Our closest neighbor was about a mile away. I am the oldest of twelve kids.

My father was always worried and complaining because the soil in Morozan was poor, so he decided we should all move to Belfate where some of his other family had gone for work. He didn't care that I had just started school, completing one-half year of first grade before we moved. Education wasn't important to him...only work that brought in money was of value. Our family then moved back and forth from Morozan to Belfate many times...making schooling very difficult. I did eventually finish third grade. My father didn't care about education for girls, saying I was only learning to write notes to lovers. This is what every father in Honduras believes.

In Belfate, we didn't have very good living conditions, sharing a pig sty with the pigs until my father could make us a house of mud. Our house in Yoro was a mud house, but we never had to share it with the animals.

When I was seven years old, I began doing the wash, cooking, and cleaning for the entire family. I would start work at 3:00 AM so that all the tortillas could be made by the time everyone else got up. I liked making tortillas and enjoyed having this quiet time alone, so this didn't bother me. We ate eggs, beans, and tortillas daily. We didn't have rice to eat, so that wasn't part of our diet like most people think.

There wasn't any time for fun and games in my life. I cared for the younger kids. Sometimes the family would go off to the beach, leaving me to do the cooking and work. I really didn't mind not going to the beach since it gave me time to work without pressure. My mother felt the need to discipline me lots when she was around. She hit me for not doing the work the way she wanted. She didn't hit the other kids, just me. I am not sure why she was always mad at me. The family was expected to help with the bean harvest in the mountains. I really didn't like this work, so would try to do my other chores slowly, in hopes of getting out of going with the family to do the beans. Sometimes this worked, other times it didn't.

My sisters and brothers and I would go to church each Sunday. My mother went three times per week. We attended the Catholic church in Morozan. My father never attended, but expected us to go.

My aunt from Yoro saw that my mother was hard on me, and asked if I could come live with her for a year. That is where I met Jose Marco and moved in with him. Marco was a good man and we were very much in love and had a wonderful relationship. His family had a small coffee finca where he also grew corn. Our first daughter was born in Yoro. Marco was a good husband and father. When his father died, we moved to Trujillo where Marco's brother lived. Marco cut wood on a mahogany

Hilda with her dolls at the store

Hilda and her soft sculpture nativity

plantation. Life was good. We had work, a place to live, and a beautiful two year old little girl I was three months pregnant with our second child, when Marco died.

At 6:00 PM a car hit him from behind as he was riding his bike on the road. They say the driver was high on marijuana. Marco had just left me at my work at Bahia Bar, saying he had an errand to do and would be back for me later. As he rode off, I had a strange feeling that things weren't quite right, but didn't understand that this was the last time I would see Marco. I was surprised when Marco's brother found me at work and told me about the accident. I went to the hospital where they told me they were going to take Marco to La Ceiba for a kidney transplant. He died before this could happen. I don't remember anything after that. I still try to remember, but just can't…it is like a piece of my life was cut away. I don't even remember giving birth to my second daughter.

I began working as a maid cleaning houses and cooking for students in Trujillo. My daughters went to live with my mother in Belfate. One night I was waiting for a taxi to go back home, when a guy came by and stopped to talk to me. He continued to do this daily for two months, even riding me home on his bike some days. Eventually I moved in with Chino. He is a kind man and is good with the kids…when he is not drunk. But when he is drunk, he hits me and grabs my hair. For safety, often I have taken the kids to his mother and then run and hidden in the woods until he is passed out. The mosquitoes eat me alive, but I have no other place to go.

I heard about a craft group here in Trujillo that was helping people learn skills and make things to sell. My cousin lives nearby and taught me how to make small bowls and things from clay. I bake them in my oven while I am cooking our rice and beans. My other nephew is part of the same craft group, Made In Honduras. He told me that if I could come up with something to make, I could join the group too. Diane is a gringa working with the group. She helped me for years trying to perfect my skills into salable items. She has helped me learn to sew dolls, and soft sculpture fish, and nativity sets. But I never had sewn before, so this was new. My nativity sets are my best product and selling well. All of this brings in a little money for food for my family. I am amazed at all the things the tourists will buy. All we have to do is think of it and make it well, then they come and buy it. I like working my two days per month in the store. It is a beautiful, airy place, filled with creative things that the other artists have made. I love being part of this group and being creative. I am always being challenged to learn something new. It is nice to have the respect and trust of everyone in the group. They voted me vice president of the group this year.

I want to have a good life with Chino, but realize it might not be possible. For self-preservation, somedays I would like to leave Chino, but am afraid to do so because he says he will hunt me down and kill me. My life is not calm. I never know when he will be drunk. I sleep with one eye open, never resting well. I live in a nice cement house that Chino built with his money, so he feels it is his. I guess I would like to build a house of my own for my daughters to have something if I am gone. Things continue to be rough. I really wish he would stop drinking permanently. This is my biggest hope for the future. I talked to him about all of this. He has promised to stop drinking… many times. He is a good man and really wants his kids to see a good example in him. It has been four months now that Chino has not been drunk. Of course having no money to spend helps this. I will always live each day

Hilda with her clay pots and soft sculpture fish

Hilda with more dolls

worrying that I will return home to a drunk man again.

We have three sons and one daughter together. I lost one son to Chino last year when the baby was born without a brain. It died when it was born. I was devastated to give birth to this dead baby. Doctors said I needed more folic acid in my diet to prevent this happening. My sister delivered two babies with the same problem. I am trying to take my vitamins with this pregnancy, but am sick a lot, so haven't been too successful as of yet.

Hilda, Chino, and kids

Juana's Story

Juana with her crystal bracelets and embroidered cards at the craft shop

I am Juana Marina Fuentes de Licona, but I only use de Licona in the church and nowhere else. I was born in Suyapita, in Orlancho on December 26, 1970. Suyapita was a large village of about 2000 people living in mud huts with tile roofs. We had no running water or septic. I lived with my parents and three brothers. We had no toys...just us. My father planted rice and beans for us and for other families who paid him what they could. My mother took care of the house and taught me to do that too. I was never real close to her. She punished without feeling, unlike my father who punished with love. It was a good lesson for me on how to treat my own children.

When I was two years old, my father accepted Christ into his heart. This changed his life and what he expected of us. Two years later, my mother became a Christian too. Papi was very strict, making us go to church on Sunday morning for more than two hours and then again on Sunday evening...and then every night of the week. He didn't think we should embellish ourselves with jewelry or make-up nor show off our bodies in skimpy clothing, so I never grew up dressing like many of my school friends.

Once I went to another village and got my ears pierced. This was right after Papi became a believer. I was very young, but remember well his reaction. He grabbed my beautiful earrings and threw them away saying God didn't make me with decorations and paint, so I shouldn't put it on myself. I was very mad and wanted to cry because I liked those earrings very much.

I have a cousin who is two years older than me. She is a good friend. Sometimes she was allowed to stay overnight with me when we were young. I liked this because I really wished I had a sister. Saturdays all of us would do the wash, iron clothes, clean house, and cook because we couldn't do these things on Sunday.

When I was five, I was visiting my great grandfather. He thought I was so pretty and took me into a room alone. He pulled up my dress and had out his penis in his hand, rubbing it on me. I had no idea what was going on nor what to do about this… after all, he was my relative whom I was supposed to give respect, right? Just then, my mother came running into the room and grabbed me away from him. I was completely surprised at all of this, and never thought about being afraid of my grandfather until this happened. My mother saved me from worse things, I know now.

At six years old I started school. I loved my teacher in first grade…and refused to move on to second grade…so they let me repeat first. Then we moved to Trujillo where my uncles were working. Papi hoped to find work too. He was a master carpenter and builder, but steady work is hard to find in Honduras. We stayed for three years and then returned to Orlancho. I went to one year of middle school and my papi took me out because he thought I was boy-crazy. (I was. I had many boyfriends from age thirteen on…) He was building houses outside the village, and gave me the job of making tortillas for everyone at 4:00 AM. I became the chief cook and housekeeper for our family and my three brothers. My mother worked as the cook at the local Day Care Center.

I led a very normal life until I was sixteen years old. Without warning, I came down with a fever and horrible pain all over my body. I was in this pain for years. Finally I just cried all the time and asked God to take me away. I knew my life was over. I would never be able to marry. Nobody could help me with the pain I was in. My parents had to do everything for me. They carried me to church, they bathed me, they put me to bed, and dressed me. I couldn't do anything for myself.

I met Angel at church. He is three years older than me and comes from a rough family, who robbed, killed, lied, and had a lot of enemies. Angel came to the church drunk with his girlfriend every week. She was afraid of his family and eventually left him. He and I talked at church. I liked him, but never thought I could have any relationship with him or anyone else due to my illness. But he liked me too, and was willing to change his ways and be part of our family. He talked to my father about marrying me. I was thrilled and scared since I was so sick. I couldn't even bathe myself due to the pain. How could I marry someone? My father wanted us to be sure of the commitment we would be making. We waited nine months before I decided to become his girlfriend...and then three years more to actually marry. I was still in great pain constantly.

But that pain was nothing as compared to the next pains that would come my way. I delivered our first baby breech...and dead. It was horrible and very painful. But that dear baby cured me of my illness. It left with the baby. I don't know how or what happened, but after this birth, I was no longer in the pain I had been in for years. I got pregnant again and a year after my first baby died, I delivered our son...a microcephalic whom the doctors thought would not live long. He lived four years with constant care from doctors and Angel and me. It was a very stressful time. We had to move to Tegucigalpa so that we could be near the hospital and doctors. Angel sold fish there and planted rice and beans for others. We had just enough money to get by. I was sick with sorrow when our son died. In some ways I am still mourning him. Then I was pregnant with twins. This was bitter sweet because again, one died...but my daughter lived. She is the joy of my life.

Things were not real calm in Orlancho. The cook where my father was working was chasing him. She really wanted him to live with her. My three brothers were drinking and getting into mischief. Then two guys were fighting outside our house. A bullet entered my mother's room and came thru the wall to my room. It ricocheted around over my head, over my daughter and my nephew. We knew it was time to get out of this place, so we moved back to Trujillo.

Juana and daughter Seleni

This time in Truillo, Papi landed a job as a watchman on a beach property. We had a place to live and a little cash. He also worked construction jobs when he could find them. But jobs were scarce. Angel couldn't find anything. Nor could my brothers. It was a tough time. We pooled all our money to send Angel to the States illegally. He made it and has been working there in New Orleans for years, sending us money to build a house. (I wish he would come home). I have been in charge of the construction. My father did the foundation and walls before he died. I have been slowly getting it into a livable condition. I love it. We have three airy bedrooms, a living room (without furniture), and a kitchen and bathroom.

I am part of a craft group in Trujillo, making bracelets and earrings. I used my profits to put on the roof of the house. I am hoping Angel will come home soon. He keeps thinking he will come, but then decides a few more months of money would be helpful. But I am lonely for him. And he hardly knows his daughter. It is my greatest hope for the future that I won't have to live it alone always, but I know better than most that God is in control of the plans He has for my life.

Juana and Seleni

Lucia's Story

Luci sewing on her treadle machine

I am Marta Lucia Zuniga. I was born in the mountains of Santa Barbara in western Honduras in 1973. The day I was born, the man who ran from the house was my father...he had three other daughters to this woman and certainly didn't need another one. So I never knew him. My mother did her best making ends meet in our mud and grass hut. She cooked and washed for food...never got real money for her work.

When I was two, my mother found a new man. He didn't like me. I was still so young that at night I often peed in the hammock. This man would slice down the hammock with his machete, crashing me to the floor. My mother was horrified, but also afraid to be alone again. Things got worse. This man would beat me for being cute. He would pound me with rocks...he even broke open my head twice. Once with a rock...I still have a huge scar and dent, and once with a board where they had to stitch the back of my head shut. I am filled with scars from his beatings and kickings and tortures. When I would see him coming down the road I would begin crying...making matters worse. He took me and put me on the grate over a fire once. That was all my mother could stand. So we finally left him...but not before my mother had had two more kids to him. One was very sick and taken to the hospital in San Pedro Sula where he died. This man would not even let my mother go get the body. He was evil. I was so happy to leave him and go to live with some relatives in Santa Rosa de Copan.

Again, my mother worked for food. And again, she found a new man. This guy was only a little better than the last. He also didn't like me. I am not sure why. I was a quiet child....and by now I was not peeing the bed. But my mother was afraid to be alone in life. She had three more children

35

with this guy. He was very strict with all of us. When I was five we moved to Satuye, near La Ceiba, where this guy got us a better house and some land to farm. He raised rice and corn, and did spraying of insecticide for other folks. We kids were not to leave the house for any reason except school and church. I got beat a good bit because I would talk to friends on the way home from school, or stop at their houses. One time after church all the other kids decided to go swimming and begged me to come along. I hesitated only a little and then took my little sisters and brothers with me to the creek. Nobody actually swam because the water was raging. But while we were there, my mother's man passed by and saw us. I got beat for everyone. His beatings were mild compared to what I had already lived through, but I did wonder why men didn't like me.

At fourteen, I ran off with Egiberto. You wonder why? Egiberto moved to Satuye with his parents when he was twenty-six. He was kind, handsome, twelve years older than me, had three kids to one woman, and 1 to another...both in another part of Honduras. His mother didn't like their influence, so she brought Egiberto with their family to Satuye. They bought a small farm there to grow rice and beans. Egiberto showed

Making dinner in her kitchen

Luci making bags   *Luci's great bags for sale*

me attention when I would pass going to school. (I was surprised that a man would like me.) He and I made a plan to elope and get me out of the house for good. I don't know what we were thinking, but we eloped in the middle of the night and went to Egiberto's house…not far down the road. My mother came looking for me and dragged us both to the Justice of Peace, who promptly put Egiberto in jail and sent me home…where I got beat. I cried for two days thinking about Egiberto being in jail because of me. My mother talked to me and decided to get Egiberto out of jail if I promised to get married to him. Of course I promised. So that night, Egiberto and I ran off again…to his parents' house. Nobody came looking for us. Nobody bothered us again from my family. My mother's man never would talk to me again, referring to me as a woman without morals.

Egiberto and I lived with his family for four months while he built us a small house on the corner of their land. It was a 1 room mud hut with a thatched roof. And for the first time in my life I was not being beat. But I was pregnant. Egiberto got drunk frequently, leaving me alone to deal with life. He also started spending time with other women. I felt terrible, but by then I had more of his kids. We now have five kids together, four daughters and one son. (I didn't see my son for three

years because Egiberto sent him away to live
with his sister. Our son was getting to the age
where he wanted to run with other youth
instead of doing his school work. So, Egiberto
decided to move him from our village to
break the pattern...but it broke my heart,
too.) Egiberto, the kids, and I had to move
when his father and mother sold their finca.
We moved to Agua Dulce, near my mother,
and rented a place there. We heard about
a land movement that was being planned
for peasants to move onto some land near

Luci and grandson

Trujillo. We joined the meetings, gave our money, time, and work, so
that we could get some land of our own some day.

On the day of the move, a big rastra (large, brightly painted, cattle
or orange delivery truck) loaded us and our belongings in the back
with lots of other families and their things. We took our chickens, a
bed, our dishes, and clothes. We had never been to the area where we
were moving, but were filled with hope for the future...and fear of the
unknown. We arrived and had to sleep under the stars on the ground.

A days work at the sewing center with Silvia

This part of the pastureland was filled with ants, so we were eaten alive by morning! Quickly we built a mud and grass hut with a thatch roof and mud floor. So life was not comfortable. Nor safe. Many rich landowners in the area of Trujillo were claiming this land was theirs. They shot at us, trying to move us off the land as we arrived. It was a scary invasion. There were 10,000 of us who eventually moved our village to another part of the land, where we are presently living. I now have a wooden slab house with a cement floor, running water, an outhouse, and just this year got electricity. It has been a long hard road, but maybe life is turning better. Egiberto no longer runs around with other women… although he still gets drunk too often.

I am part of a sewing group in our village. We make beautiful bags and other items that we sell in the craft co-op in Trujillo. I am a very good seamstress because I am very particular about my work. I have learned in life that it is best not to make mistakes. I have been very careful to protect my children so that they won't have the fears and bad things in life that I had. I encourage them to be good students and study for some profession so that they can have a future to work towards. Besi, our oldest, just had our first grandson. So life continues and I pray that God will bless my children.

Luci, Egiberto, and family

Luz's Story

Luz with her products

I am Luz. My real name is Maria Luz Padilla. I am the ninth of ten kids in the family and was born on February 25th, 1978 in Guayapa, Orlancho. We all lived in a large mud house with a tile roof that belonged to the landowner. It had four bedrooms, kitchen, and living room. We had no electric or plumbing. We all had to haul the family water daily. We were a happy family that didn't fight like so many other families did.   My mother made tortillas and sold them. She also sewed for people. My father helped with the bean harvest on area farms. We had no toys...just played with the bottles on the road. When I was five years old, my parents sent us to a day care center that opened in our village. My parents picked rice and beans nearby and we played all day. I loved playing ball. I also loved being the princess in a play at school. I got to wear a beautiful pink dress that my mother had a lady make for me. It was my favorite dress ever. That is when I met Adam. We have been girlfriend and boyfriend since we were six years old. He has always been there for me.

The day care center paid for all of us to go to school, buying our books and uniforms. Without this help, I would not have been able to study as long as I did since my parents had no extra money for education. I was in ninth grade when the center closed, leaving us stranded. I had no way of continuing my classes and was devastated. My life changed with that center closing. I had spent all my free time with friends, going to the park for ice cream or just hanging out. Now that would end too.

When I left school I had to look for work. I went to Tegucigalpa where my sister lived, hoping to find something there. Adam also went to Teguc looking for work. I found a job watching two kids while their mother worked. I lived with my sister for three years, making L.800 per month (that is about forty dollars now). I helped my mother with money and paid for food for my sister. When that job ended, I returned to Orlancho to live with my parents. Adam came from Teguc for me...we missed each other and ran off together in secret for Trujillo where his family lived. We lived with them for a few months until we built a place of our own. My parents were mad, like all Honduran parents when their kids run off, but they eventually settled down. After all, they had known Adam for a lifetime.

Adam had jobs in construction. He built us a small cement house where our first son was born. Then Mitch hit Honduras with raging winds and water that took our land away. It took the roof off of the house, so we had to move into a mud hut. Many programs came in after the hurricane giving us food, but we suffered for two years till we had a life again. Now, slowly, we are getting our house made again. It is made of cement now with a thatch cabana in front where people who come to our store can sit and drink sodas and beer. I opened this store with money I got from selling things in the craft co-op. We needed money and food...a store seemed like a good idea. It is hard to have a store in Honduras because everyone wants to buy on credit. You have to be tough and stand up for what you know you have to do to keep a good business running. I think I am successful. It is not hard to get to our house since it is right along the main road into Trujillo. We built it on land that is the green strip along the road. There was no other land available, and many families were settling in this area, so we did too. We add a room to it as we get the money. Since we are at the bottom of the hill out to the road, we have big drainage puddles to jump over or wade thru to get into our store and house. Recently Adam bought an old taxi for us to use as a family car. We keep it in front of our house, giving us some extra privacy.

Eight years after our son was born, we had a daughter. I am glad I can stay home with the children

Luz making pretty necklaces at home

Luz with her magnets and earrings

since the store is at our house. I love my children. The happiest days of my life were when they were born. The saddest day was just this year when my brother died of a heart attack. He was so young.

I have dreams. I would like to have a clothing store. I think I have good taste in clothing and could get nice things to sell. But this takes more money than we have right now. I do enjoy making jewelry and could sell it with the clothing...someday.

I entered the craft group after hearing about it from Adam's sister and family. I watched for a while to see if this was a good thing or not... so many groups come and go and promise and leave. But this group seemed honest and worth looking into. I am now president of the group. I began by making wooden fish and keyholders with Adam. Now I make mainly beaded necklaces. I hope people continue to like my products so I can continue making them.

God has watched over me and my family. My life is calm and good.

Luz, Adam, and their kids

Maira's Story

Maira making her recycled plastic bag purses

Hola! I am Maira Aguilar. Born on November 12, 1981 in Lorencito, Sonaguera, Colon. I am the oldest of seven girls and two boys. Our family lived like all the other families I knew, in a one-room mud house with a thatch roof. We partitioned off the sleeping area with sheets. I spent my childhood helping my mother with the other kids. When I was about six years old, we moved to Orlanchito looking for work. My father rented land for a milpa* and planting yucca. My next sister and I worked with him in his milpa everyday before school. We helped him plant rice and beans on his rented land. He had huge success and was known for his good crops. This made many people envious of him. They would put their horses in the milpa to ruin it. After four years of this, we moved back to Lorencito where there was no trouble with the neighbors.

I had started school in Orlanchito, and loved it. Spanish was my favorite subject. Math was my least favorite. It was hard. At recess I played games with my friends. Our favorite was Ojitos y Cebollitas where we would all sit on our hunkers in a circle and someone would go around the outside and tap one of us on the shoulder…then we would have to run and catch them. I finished sixth grade, but had no money to go on for more schooling.

When I was sixteen, Hurricane Mitch devastated Honduras. Our family was held hostage by this storm in all its fury. We lived in a mud house with a tile roof at the time. There was a small stream flowing near the house. During the storm, the stream rose and divided all around the house, trapping us. We were scared…but not as scared as we were

*milpa: a corn patch

43

when the storm blew all the tiles off the roof. The rain pelted us. The wind blew through our walls. We were all soaked and so was everything we owned. Trees were falling all around the house…and on the house. All of us were petrified. When the wind subsided some, we made our way thru the water and rain to my grandmother's house. There we rode out the storm. Thank goodness she had dry clothes that we all wore whether they were too big or were for a woman or not, we didn't care. It felt good to be dry and secure with family all around on this terrible day.

After the storm, the land my father had around the house was gone… it was now a new stream. He had no place to plant new crops…and all the old ones were washed away. Life looked pretty bleak at this point. But God always gives you an opening to continue on in life. I heard about this land movement that was forming to move to some land that the government set aside for peasants. The movement was offering land, cattle projects, education, and security for the future. You just had to pay an entrance fee and agree to stay with the group as they entered the land. I saw this as a way to have a future, a house of my own, and a job all in one package. My father and mother also thought this was a great option since they now had nothing. But I had no money. So I went to San Pedro Sula to get work in a maquila (sweat shop). The one where I found work made shirts. They put me on the inspection line. Thousands of shirts passed by me everyday. I worked from 7:00 AM to 6:00 PM and was paid about twenty dollars per six day week, From this pay, I needed to rent a room and get food. I would walk to and from my job, even though it was far, but this way I didn't need to waste money on a taxi or bus. I saved every penny I could for paying my entrance fee.

When I had finally saved enough to pay my fee, I got news from my parents that the movement was starting and that I should return to help pack up our belongings. This was such an exciting time, full of hope and promise. (Nobody ever mentioned that there were ranchers using this same land and that they would not be happy to see us coming. I never dreamed of all the stress and fighting that would ensue.) I helped my mother pack up our clothes and our pots and pans. We climbed onto the big cattle truck that came by for us and about fifteen other families. We rode in the pouring rain to the area that is now called Guadalupe Carney. Our procession of 10,000 people arrived between 10:00 PM and 1:00 AM, with ranchers shooting at us from nearby hills. We didn't come with arms, only machetes. We came in trucks, pick-ups, horseback, and on foot. We were all filled with hope and dreams...and now scared, but now had nothing to return to, as most of us had spent our last pennies to get here. I was sure we were all going to die that night. But nobody was hurt or killed, thanks to God. In the morning we began building our mud huts and grass roofs. We also took food with us from our home, figuring there might not be any there for a few days. As it turned out, very few others brought food along, and there was none to be had anywhere except for us. There were no stores nearby and we were not welcomed in the area even if there were, so nobody could get food...except for what we brought with us. Needless to say, our supply didn't last very long.

Immediately the energy of the village movement began. Everyone had a job to do getting this organized. I was assigned to part of the Education Committee. We built a small school house over a cement slab that was already on the land. This stick and vine-wall and thatch roof building housed all the kids in the village who could fit. Our committee of five were responsible for teaching the kids and also for securing a permanent teacher. I loved my new job and working with the kids to give them a future. Two teachers eventually came after about two months. One was from our movement, the other from Trujillo. The government paid these teachers. Since the rules of the movement said you couldn't be part of a government program and the movement too, the teacher from the village had to decide which she wanted...free land or a job. She chose the job and had to move away.

After a year of trying to make a settlement on this land, we decided to move across the road to more favorable land. The area where we were originally settled was filled with army ants and fire ants. Everything we planted was eaten overnight and we were miserable with fire ant bites. We got government help to

Maira learning her craft

build a new school on the new village land. We also got more teachers. A program was offered for me to continue in my schooling, but my empressa* wouldn't give me permission to leave my work with them. I worked daily cutting grass and planting palms. Since I had no husband or partner, I had to do all the hours myself.

After a few years, I got the empressa to give me permission to attend school in the afternoons, and I would work for them every morning. I finished six more years of schooling this way. It was the happiest day of my life when I received my diploma. My mother and sister came to the ceremony. When I graduated, I met Francisco. He also was part of the village movement, so I had seen him around. He moved into my house with his one daughter. He has other kids in Orlancho, but doesn't see them often. Francisco and I have a daughter now, Tanya Joselin Rameriz Aguillar. We are committed to helping the village survive, and to giving our children a future. We work hard daily in the palms on our empressa's land. The rancher who was living there, had no titles to the land, but says he does. He has been fighting our empressa for eight years. We had agreed to pay him for his palms and fencing as we got money. He got mad when we used our money from the palm harvest to buy a truck to help with getting the palm fruit to the factory. So this rancher had our truck impounded. Francisco was furious, but what could we do? Our empressa had been taking turns every day for eight years, sleeping on the land to make sure this guy knew it was ours. One night in August of 2008, the rancher sent five armed men in to kill us. We all scattered, but he did kill one of our people, and injured another. We ran to the police asking for help, but they wouldn't do anything because this rancher has lots of powerful friends and is himself a police commissioner in another part of the country. At this point, some of the villagers went to the house of the rancher and surrounded it. Then a terrible thing happened: someone set fire to the house, killing all the people inside. This has infuriated the rancher, making life miserable for our entire village. This was a terrible thing to do, and I wish it wouldn't have happened. But it does not change how I feel about our village. Francisco and I are committed to staying and helping with getting the land titles. The government has been very slow in giving us our titles, but we will get them. This is our future.

Having said all of this, I want to let you know that the land is not

*empressa: a community co-op

the most important thing in my life. God is. It is through Him that everything is given to us. All opportunities are from Him. One amazing opportunity presented itself to me in being part of the craft group, Made In Honduras. I had learned to crochet from my mother and would always be making little bags and giving them to friends and family. I wanted to enter the youth group in the village, but they didn't have a spot for me to work with them. So I approached the missionary in charge of the craft group that was forming and showed her my bags. Diane told me to bring the things to a sale on her porch and see if they were a good item to sell. The team of people who passed through bought them and I began making more and more bags for the store. Then another person came and taught me how to crochet snowflakes. Now I make angels and am trying to make a crocheted nativity set. I also crochet table runners and tablecloths. My newest product is layered necklaces crocheted with tiny beads in them. Very pretty. All this might seem small to you, but it has given me a job of my own. With my baby and my other work at the house and for the empressa, I am very busy. But I feel this opportunity with the craft group is also a good future for me. It is money for food once in a while. The group voted me president for last year. It has been my privilege to lead them. I am also part of a silk scarf painting group that meets once a week. We make beautiful scarves of many colors and designs.

God continues to give us guidance in this life. I would never have dreamed of all the fighting and turmoil that these last few years would bring, but in the midst of all of this, He has blessed me with a daughter, and hard-working man, and a job that offers me hope for the future.

Maira drawing blood from her cow

Maria's Story

Maria with her sea glass angels

My name is Maria Magdalena Ramirez Orellana...but all my friends and family call me Maria. I am twenty-five years old and the mother of one baby girl and two little boys, Samuel who is eight, and Ariel who is three years. My partner is Alexis Chacon. Ale and I are not married, but have been together since we were seventeen. We have known each other all our lives since we are both from the same area of Yoro, high in the mountains of Honduras. Ale wants to get married, but I am not sure. I have seen so many men run off and leave their women. I don't want to be tied to anyone who might do that...but I don't think Ale would leave us. He loves his kids and me.

I was born in a board house with a tin roof, just like all eight of my brothers and sisters. My father has a small coffee finca that my mother and older siblings helped work with him when we were growing up. He started with two cows that were left to him when his father died. Those grew and had enough calves that he sold to buy the small coffee finca. Our village has about thirty houses...most are the same as my family's house, some are adobe. Now that my father is selling his coffee in our craft store, he is making more money and has built my mother an adobe house too. It even has more than one room!

I remember when I was small I had the job of caring for my younger siblings while my mother and father were in the finca. This was a big responsiblilty...and if I didn't do something right, or one of the kids got hurt, my mother would beat me with a rubber belt from on old car. She had put nails in the end of it, so it tore up my skin. At ten, I graduated from being the main watch person for the kids to the main cook for the workers on the finca. Everyday I would make their beans and tortillas, or eggs, or beans and spaghetti. If I made too many tortillas, my mother would beat me with the car belt; if I made too few tortillas, my mother would beat me with the car belt. My mother has changed, but in those days it was the only way she knew to do discipline. To her credit, she taught me how to sew. Every year after the coffee harvest, my mother would go to Morozan and buy two yards of fabric for each of us to make a new dress. If you made any mistake, you had to live with it until the next year!

I had never been to school because my family could not afford to send me, even though I wanted to learn to read and write badly. Another woman in the village knew my desire and began to teach me. But my visits were scattered since I was not to leave the house and seldom had any chance to do so. But I would practice what she had taught me...and every chance I got, I tried more. My father saw me trying to write, and would correct me and show me new words. But he had sent my first four brothers and sisters to school and they all left not knowing anything, so my father was not about to waste more money on me. (Here in Honduras parents pay to send their kids to public school, plus they have to buy uniforms, shoes, books, paper and pens. It comes to about fifty dollars per year per student. Most peasants don't have anything near that in expendable income.)

It was around the time I was twelve or thirteen that I had been walking down the road from our village and a man whom I didn't know beckoned me to come over to him. He talked really nice to me and asked me to show him something in the bushes. I was a bit confused, but didn't want to be rude, so went with him. He took my hand and pulled me with him faster, then began to grope at me. I was scared to death, not knowing what he was doing. Just then, my neighbor passed by and called to me. The man ran off. I never saw him again...thank goodness. But I will remember this forever. I never told my mother because I knew she would beat me, even though I didn't do anything wrong.

Maria with her dad and his coffee

When I was fourteen, Hurricane Mitch hit Honduras. In my village the devastation

Maria and Ale celebrating their graduation from 6th grade

was not so bad, like the rest of our country. Since we lived high in the mountains, we didn't have the terrible floods. We did have some mud slides, but nobody was killed. The day before the storm hit, my parents had gone to the clinic in Morazan with my younger brother who was very sick with pneumonia. They left me in charge of all the other kids at the house. My parents got stranded at the clinic for two days because of the hurricane, and were very worried about us. When they tried to walk back up the mountain to our house, they couldn't get across the raging river to our village, and had to walk another two days around to get there. There were no telephones or radios in our village at that time, so communication was impossible. My parents were panicked to know we were alone in this horrible storm. Our neighbors were constantly running over to the house to check on us kids. We were scared to death as the winds blew from every direction and rains pounded the house. Our roof flapped in the wind, but didn't blow away like some.

After the hurricane, the leaders of our community got together and brought a truckload of food to us. It was interesting...there were beans in cans. We had never heard of such a thing. But we ate them...we were hungry. They also gave each family a few cans of meat. It was so tender and tasted so good...until someone told us it was horse meat. Then we all threw every can of it out. It seemed possible since none of us had ever eaten anything that was so tender and flavorful. There was some writing on the can...in English, so nobody knew what it said. (I have since learned about canned beef, and am sure that is what we threw out!) The truck also had used clothing for us. Since none of us had lost any clothing, it was unusual for us to be given this, we thought. But a gift is a gift, so we all gathered around the truck, sorting through the clothes. People from the USA had sent their best to us...all kinds of things we didn't

Reading with Samuel

know what to do with. Bathing suits...what on earth would you do with this thing (when we swim, we go in our clothes)? We would hold them up laughing, trying to figure out what it was for...and finally decided to cut the bottom off and use them for tops.

One year my family went to the local school for the annual Mother's Day Activities. I saw Ale, who was a student in the school. He looked so handsome in his navy pants and white shirt uniform. And he seemed to be looking at me too. He visited me a few times after this. When he graduated from sixth grade, we decided to run off together...to his house. We were both seventeen. To me it seemed like a good opportunity to get out of the house. Here was this good looking guy who liked me and wasn't requiring me to do tons of work. I was not sure Ale was going to be a good provider or if he would even stay with me, but at least I was not going to be beat anymore and could work for myself. We lived with Ale's folks for eight days until we could build a small house of sticks and grass on their land. By then I was pregnant with Samuel. Ale tried helping out on the finca and looking for other work in the area, but there just isn't anything extra in Yoro. And now we were going to have another mouth to feed.

Maria and Samuel making sea glass crosses

Many of our cousins, aunts, and other family had gone to Trujillo over the years, to get work. So we thought we would give it a try too. There certainly was no hope of work in San Augustine or anyplace close by. We arrived in Trujillo when Samuel was eighteen months old, with only a small backpack that had a bottle for Samuel and a small bag of powdered milk, three dresses for me, one set of clothes for Ale, a plate, cup and spoon, and a small blanket.

We lived with various family members for a few months at a time, as is the custom here until we could get settled. Some shared their food with us, some didn't. We often went without food, and would gladly have returned to Yoro if we had the bus fare. Ale tried to get work everyday, but had little luck. He was determined to take care of us. He worked in a grocery store…for thirty dollars per month. He worked loading cement blocks on a truck for two dollars per day. He tried his hand at many things…none of which were more than a few days of pay at a time. This is very common in Honduras. He eventually took a job with a neighbor making charcoal. This is the dirtiest, lowest job a peasant can find. After cutting the sticks, digging a hole, layering the sticks with leaves and grass to burn slowly, and covering it all to simmer for days, Ale would ride his bike all over creation trying to sell his charcoal to the restaurants in the area. After all of this, Ale would go looking for firewood for us so that I could cook our rice and tortillas. Some days he was just too tired to look for wood and we wouldn't eat. One day the gringa, Diane, who lived across the road brought me some of her left over taco salad that she said would go bad if we didn't eat it right away.

Maria in her kitchen with Diane

I remember thanking her, and wondering how she could possibly have known that we had been without food for three days. I tried to wait for Ale to come home to eat this salad. But Samuel and I were so hungry that we had to eat before him. It was the best food...a new taste to my mouth. We did save some for Ale too.

We lived in a small eight by ten foot structure that we put used pieces of tin over to have a roof. We held the tin on with blocks and rocks. We had no water or electricity or plumbing. It was an old, rotting block structure sitting on the property of a landowner who lives in Italy. So we agreed to live on her land until she came. This is not unusual for Honduras. Most peasants here have no land or house or toilet...we just use the bushes or grass in the yard when we need to. A watchman on the property near us let us run an extension cord from his light bulb to our house so we could have light at night. We even eventually bought a refrigerator that we ran off of that extension cord. Thinking of it now, it is a wonder that nobody got zapped with that plan, as the cord was only buried about two inches under the dirt on the road where cars passed daily, and water stood in the rains.

At this same time, I got to know Diane and Scott better. After all I did have to return her bowl. She invited me into the nicest house I was ever in, and made me feel quite at ease. So I went to visit her

Maria with the cake she made at Diane's fifty-fifth birthday

Selling at craft exhibit

on another day when I saw her outside. She was always making something. She had taught other people along the beach to make things, so I was hoping she could give me something to make too. I told her I liked to sew and asked if she had any ideas for me. She did! We bought some old second hand tropical-print shirts and I sewed them into squeegees for your hair. Our friends were selling their crafts to workteams and medical teams that passed through the area. I was hoping to break into this market, and sewed up a storm to have product to sell to the next team that came thru. But to my dismay, nobody bought any! I was so disappointed. But Diane didn't give up on me and promised that I could find something to make and sell. So I kept trying. She taught me to paint on rocks. She had made a few door stops for her house and other people were wanting some. So I practiced on sheets of paper that she lined all around her kitchen counters. Amazingly, I eventually learned how to draw and even use a paint brush. I made seventeen rocks with iguanas on them for an order for another gringo for Christmas presents. He paid me about fifty cents per rock. It was more money than I had ever seen! Then I expanded to making small village houses out of the rocks. Again, this was Diane's idea, but I was learning that she had ideas that people would buy. The team members seemed to like taking a village house back home with them. Over a year they bought enough houses that I could buy a gas stove, so Ale wouldn't have to look for firewood every day. We still laugh when we think that our stove was bought with rocks! I also began painting Christmas cards, sewing sun visors and hats, and then came the real surprise: sea glass jewelry. Yes, gringos go crazy over sea glass. Garbage that the sea spits back onto the beaches...I collect it and wrap it with wire and make it into necklaces and earrings. I am a member of a small craft co-op that sells these items, making it possible for me to send Samuel to school in Trujillo.

We had to move from the tiny house we had created on the borrowed land when a neighbor began bothering us at night wanting money. So we took the job as watchmen at the new store for the co-op. We don't get paid anything, and still have to pay our electricity, but we have a nice, big (two bedrooms) apartment below the store to live in. I am the administrator at the store...mainly because we live there, and I can do math better than most of the other folks in the craft group. Because of this job, I have learned to do math even better. My reading and writing is improving too. I went to school at night for two years and graduated from sixth grade. I am now in seventh grade, taking classes every Saturday. It is tons of work and homework. Diana is helping me since there is lots I really don't understand. The teacher gives us a packet of papers and says to learn it. It is hard to teach yourself English, multiplication and division. I plan to continue on and maybe someday will be a teacher or an accountant.

Ale and I have saved our money together to buy a small coffee finca in Yoro in the mountains above our parents. We go there once a year to harvest the coffee and visit the family. Ale has spent lots of time this past year building a house for us. I picked the plans off of the internet. It is an adobe house with a tin roof. It has four bedrooms...one of which I plan to use for my craft work. It is nice to have this security for the future. I am amazed at how God has guided me and saved me and taught me over the years. He has given me many blessings...especially my wonderful children, Ale, and friends.

Maria, Ale and family

56 A WALK IN MY SHOES

Marlin's Story

Marlin and her products

My name is Marlin Osiris Aguilar-Guevara. March 25, 1990, I was born in the mountain village of Lorencito near Sonaguera in Colon, Honduras. Our family lived in a mud and thatch hut, like all the other houses in our area. I have two brothers, and am the middle child. My father was a subsistence farmer, planting corn and beans on a small piece of land that his brother gave him. It was just enough land for our family to barely survive. My father would always divide the harvest into two piles... one for us to eat, and the other to sell in market, so that he could buy more seeds for the next crop. It was my job to help him harvest the beans and corn. I also had the regular household chores of getting water, making tortillas, and washing clothes.

I loved school and was a good student. In fact, I was smart enough to get a scholarship, so I didn't cost my family anything.

When I was eight, Hurricane Mitch hit our country hard. Lorencito was filled with water and mudslides. It was scary to hear the roaring wind and pounding rain for days. When it was over, we had no land to farm.

At this time we heard about a land reform movement that was forming in another part of Colon. My parents joined the group. They were all excited about the possibilities that this would offer us...land, jobs, education, programs. We couldn't wait to go to this utopia. When I was ten years old, the day finally came to leave, we loaded our few belongings and our family into the back of a big cattle truck for the trip to our new home. We were all singing and excited about this move. So when we got there and there were gun shots, I thought it was friendly ranchers welcoming us. But on the contrary! It was unfriendly ranchers warning us to go away.

So for nine years, the ranchers were fighting our group at every turn, even though the government gave us permission to be on this land. But the ranchers want the land for themselves. Many people from the village have been killed over these years in confrontations with the ranchers. None of the ranchers are ever punished because they do their killing by night when nobody can see, and also because they have money and connections to not be seen. Right now it is very hard to live calmly in the village because one powerful rancher has put out a list of villagers he wants arrested and killed. So most of our men are not leaving the village to go to any work. Therefore nobody has money to buy food. It is tough for everyone…even though most of us are not on the list. If I would have known what these years of fighting and unrest would be like, I would have chosen to stay in Lorencito where life was poor, but calm.

Those first days in the new village that we called Guadalupe Carney, were filled with fun. Many countries gave us games to play, so that we kids would be entertained while the adults were getting things organized and built. I loved the games, and played them all day long with the other kids. But the parts to the games got lost quickly.

There was only one stream in this village area. That made things difficult because there were 10,000 people that needed to bathe and wash clothes. We would stand in line for hours waiting for our turn at the stream. The men in the village eventually dug three wells that helped some. But this area was not good for settling this many people. So in a year, we all packed up everything and moved to the other side of the road where there was more space, more water, and less fire ants!

I finished sixth grade in Guadalupe Carney. And I joined the youth group that was led by volunteers from Belgium, Greet and Stef. Greet taught me so many things…how to make necklaces, earrings, dreamcatchers, rings, and more. She and Stef helped those of us in the youth group to get scholarships to continue schooling. We had a group of forty kids who participated in crafts, music, dancing, and meetings. I am the only one left of this group, since by

Marlin making her bracelet

definition, youth will grow up and turn into adults. I too have grown, but am continuing to make my crafts. I sell necklaces, earrings, and bracelets in a craft co-op. I am glad to have this opportunity to make a little money for food for our family. I have a one year old son who cries lots when he doesn't have any food. Rolando is his father, who I got to know when he was part of the music program with the youth in the village.

The happiest day of my life was when my son was born. I can't tell you how amazing this miracle of life is to me. He is precious and I thank God for him everyday.

The saddest day of my life was when I was still small and a woman killed my grandfather. She had been treating him mean for quite a while, putting her cows into our bean field. But one day, she killed him. I couldn't believe this had happened to my grandfather. It was such a shock to me. And it was an early call to the reality of violence that occurs too often in Honduras. But there is no law enforcement, so people pretty much do what they want. I will never forget the lessons of that sad day when my grandfather was killed. I am sure there is more to that story, but I never heard it. I just remember a man I loved dearly.

I live in a small mud and thatch hut in our village. Our one room serves for everything. Someday, we hope to have enough money to turn it into a cement house. Rolando and I are happy and hopeful for a good future together.

Marlin with her family at their house

Nicolasa's Story

Nicol sewing at her home

My name is Nicolasa Claderon. I was born in San Antonio, Las Crucitas, Copan on April 8th, 1966. I have three brothers and one sister. Two other babies died because they were born without any blood. We lived in a house made of tied grass. We had one bed. My mother and the two youngest slept on a patate (grass mat) on the bed. The rest of us slept on a patate under the bed. My earliest memories are of walking three or four miles to the coffee finca where my father was working to bring him his food. I learned at this early age to balance the food on my head so that my hands were free to carry other things. After I got my father's food to him, I had to carry water two miles for our family to use in the house.

When I was seven, mother bought me my first underpants. I remember this so well because I hated them. The elastic cut into my skin. I couldn't imagine why anyone would want to wear these things.

When I was eight, my father moved out of our house to live with his girlfriend. We cried lots. He would send food to us, but that was all. We couldn't go to school because there was no money to pay for the entrance fee or books and uniforms. Our mother said we would just learn to write love notes anyway, so it wasn't worth it to send us. She was so mad at being alone. She hit us lots to keep us in line. She always threatened to send us girls away since we weren't worth anything. We all sold tortillas and wood in the market to get some money…but it wasn't much, since everyone could make their own tortillas and get wood themselves.

Eventually we moved in with our grandmother in Copan. This made life a bit more comfortable and secure. At least we weren't always wondering if we would be sent away now. But Mother still had no money nor clothes for us. So she would take our father back, to get some money. Then they would fight and split again. This happened more times than I can count.

I was in charge of taking care of my younger siblings. Daily Mother would remind me to take good care of them because if they died, she would kill me! So at twelve, I was glad to have the job of cooking food for the workers at the coffee finca of my father. It didn't matter that I needed to start work at 3:00 AM. I also worked in my mother's pulperia (little store). Lots of men passed by for beer and soda and other food. But I was not allowed to talk to them at all. I got hit for looking at guys. I got hit for not being fast at my work. I got hit for not thinking fast. I had to work, work, work. I made tortillas, I cooked beans and rice, I washed clothes, I washed dishes. Life was work...and getting hit.

At seventeen, I decided life was just too much trouble to live. I figured it would be best to just end things once and for all. I threw a rope over the rafter and put the loop around my neck. Then I jumped off a chair. But the knot stuck...gagging me, instead of hanging me. So I quickly jumped back on the chair, removed the rope, and decided I wasn't going to die that day.

My father picked a worker on his finca that he liked a lot and thought I should marry. I didn't like him, so wouldn't talk to him. But every three months a soldier passed by the pulperia on his way to visit his mother. His name was Ezekiel. He was handsome and kind, and wanted to talk. But I told him I couldn't until he got permission from my father, or I'd be hit. Ezekiel was afraid of my father since he knew my father had picked another man for me. But after three more months, Ezekiel got up his nerve. He brought a suitcase full of clothes, towels, and other gifts for our family. But Mother and Father didn't want them, and gave them back. Ezekiel left and returned with two gifts for the babies, and asked to talk with me. He knew how my parents treated me and wanted me to run off with him. I was afraid to do this because my father said he would beat anyone to death with a stick if they ever touched me. So I was afraid to test this.

When I was eighteen, Ezekiel and I got married. The night before the wedding, Ezekiel brought me my first pair of pants to wear for the trip to the church. I rode a horse for four hours to El Paras so we could be married in the church. It was my first horse ride, so was not a relaxing trip. My parents would not come. Mother was pregnant again and couldn't make the trip. She cried and cried as I left with a friend who was going with me. There were nineteen other couples getting married that day, Dia de San Miguel, the 29th of September. After the wedding, Ezekiel and I went to a hotel. I wanted to stay with my friend, but she insisted I had to stay with my husband now.

We went to his parents' house for one year where he worked on their milpa (corn field). Then my father gave us a small lot in Copan where we built a little wooden house with a tile roof. We worked on the coffee finca of my father. And at twenty-two I was pregnant with our first child.

But the coffee wasn't paying, so we all had to leave….my parents, my brothers and sisters, and our new family. Our little girl was two and one-half years old. We went to Colon looking for work that we had heard was there. We went to the end of the road and then three hours up the mountain from Guadalupe. It was a trek. My father had bought eight manzanas there to plant corn. Living there was tough since we only had what we could carry with us. There was no food.

Our second child was born sick and thin. She died of a fever. Our next child lived for one year and four months. I had taken her to a doctor in Tocoa, who yelled at me and said I must go to Tegucigalpa with this sick baby. I told him I had no money to go there, and no food for her nor me. He did nothing. My daughter died there with pneumonia and heart problems.

Then Mauricio was born. He was a strong boy who always wanted to please his father, but couldn't. Ezekiel would fight him at every turn. He would hit him at every little thing. When he was thirteen I talked with Ezekiel and told him I was leaving and taking the kids if he didn't back off on Mauricio. He said he would try and took him to Tocoa on a selling trip. But

Nicolasa cooking on her mud stove

Nicolasa and Luci with their products

they returned and everything was the same. Except now he began hitting me. He would use a belt on me because I was standing up for my son. He would fight me and call me names. It was terrible. Ezekiel never did talk to Mauricio. But when Mauricio was sixteen, he went North, and Ezekiel cried and cried for all he had done and not done with his son.

One day, a priest talked to Ezekiel and told him that he had seven kids and that was enough, and that Ezekiel should do family planning His mother told him he would burn in Hell if he did family planning. This brought on more fights between us. Ezekiel heard about a land movement and wanted to join it. I had planned to leave him, but he promised to change. So we moved to Guadalupe Carney with 10,000 other people who were looking for a better life for their families.

We suffered without food or work in that first year. Then Ezekiel got a cow through a project in the village and took classes on how to care for it. He became a good farmer. I joined sewing classes and then formed a small group that makes bags to sell in a co-op. We built a nice new house of mud and thatch with mud floors and mud stove. Ezekiel takes care to plant lots of fruit trees and pineapples. We have lots of flowers around our house too. It makes us feel good that people who visit our village like to come by the house and see our garden. Ezekiel was feeling better about himself because he got to work daily when our co-op was building a store. This gave us an income and gave him importance in the family. He no longer felt like he was useless. But once that building was done, he no longer had a job. We no longer had an income. Ezekiel sold his cow to pay for school for the kids. He was feeling low again…up and down. Our missionary friends gave him another project making worm compost that we can use for our garden and can also sell. Ezekiel is content and busy with his garden. He also built us a new cement house with four bedrooms. Mauricio sent us the money to build it from his job in the US. Now we are struggling to put our other children through school. Norma is in nursing school in La Ceiba. She has many expenses for this program. Nora also wants to go to nursing school, but has to wait another year till she is old enough to enter. Our two younger sons are still in school here in the village.

Our village has its ups and downs. We worked hard for years to get our land titles from the government. We now have them, but then they were held hostage by a rich land owner who was mad at the village for burning his house and killing his family. This made things very uneasy here, since nobody felt safe and couldn't go out of the village for work. Food was scarce. Everyone was thin. We got a few relief food distributions that helped some. Now this guy is gone, and there are other political problems. Always somebody trying to fight us to get off our land. Why? We are good people. We are only trying to make a living...not get rich. We have not taken anything that wasn't due us. But there is seldom a calm day in our lives. Struggle is all we know.

But we do look to the future with hope.

Nicol, Ezikiel, and family

Norma's Story

Norma with her earrings

My name is Norma Xiomara Urrea. I was born on Sept 20th, 1987 in Copan. I am the second of six kids, so got lots of training in helping with the little ones. I was only one when we left Copan for El Union en Colon, so I don't remember much about Copan.

But the first memory I have is of my baby sister being born. She came to us with a bad heart and died at one and one-half years old. During this time my older brother and I had to care for her in the hammock to be sure she wouldn't suffocate while she was sleeping. We swung the hammock and sang to her. It was very sad when she died. Our mother took her to Tocoa to the doctor, who said she needed surgery in Tegucigalpa. We had no money for this trip let alone the hospital and medications and surgery. In fact, we had no money for food where we were. Momi told the doctor this, but he didn't help us out. In a few days my sister died. We brought the body back home for burial, and planted roses on the grave. Momi cried for days that turned into months. We were all very sad for our sister and for our mother.

Life was always a struggle. Our family had no food. Our grandmother would bring us tortillas daily from corn in her milpa. We didn't have any land to have a milpa. Papi had no money to buy land, and had no job to get any money. He just helped in the milpa of Momi's parents. This made him feel helpless about taking care of his family, and therefore he was often mad and looking for a fight with Momi.

Momi was sick for a long time after the baby died. She got an infection in her breasts that made her very ill. We took her to the hospital in Tocoa where she had to stay for a week. Of course we had no money to pay for this, so the Catholic church helped us.

We lived in a wattle and daub house with a thatch roof. It was one room for sleeping, and the other was the kitchen. We had a bed with a mattress and the rest of us slept on mats on the floor. I had a special stuffed animal rabbit that I really liked when I was little. I also had two very special dresses that Momi bought me for visiting relatives and going to church. One was pink and one was red. We went to church every Sunday morning, and to catechism every Sunday afternoon.

When I was five I started working on my grandfather's land with my father. It was my job to carry water to the other workers in the milpa. When the corn was sold, Papi would buy some material for us to all make skirts.

If I wasn't working carrying water in the milpa, I had to haul water and clean at the house, or grind corn, or wash diapers. I liked when Papi took me to pull the beans or to plant the corn because it got me out of the house.

Papi brought toys to us once, but I didn't particularly like them since I wasn't used to having them. The parts got lost and that made me not like toys even more. Birthdays weren't celebrated with toys or presents or cake. Momi just told me that she loved me lots on every birthday.

Christmas was not a celebration in our house either. In fact it was usually sad because Papi was usually mad at Momi for using so much corn to make tamales, and for being sick and needing so many medicines that he couldn't get for her. So he would fight her and call her names. This made me not really enjoy having tamales. Momi prayed lots for Papi to change his ways.

At seven, I went to first grade. My teacher told my mother that I couldn't talk right. We had never known this. Friends at school tried to help me with words that I couldn't say. It seems that my tongue was tied...it was grown to the bottom of my mouth and therefore I couldn't stick out my

Hot tortillas

Norma in her nursing uniform

tongue at all. This hindered me saying some sounds. But it made me study very hard so I could read silently very well. We didn't know this could be fixed until I was thirteen and went to another school where the teacher also noticed this problem. We found out that the surgery would cost L.500. Since this was not a life nor death situation, we didn't do anything until a few years later when we met some missionaries who helped us with the fee. They cut my tongue in Trujillo without any anesthesia or anything and sent me home. So now I can talk just fine.

At thirteen my life changed. . . . Before thirteen, I was always afraid that Papi would leave us and then what would we do? Thirteen was also when we moved to Guadalupe Carney with the land invasion. My father changed lots in this time. He became more calm about things, and didn't fight us as much. He was part of a group that gave him purpose for his life. He went to Christian Veterinary Mission's classes on how to care for cows and became a good farmer. Momi joined a sewing group and brought in a little money from this work. Then my older brother went north to the US and began sending money to us. All of this made a big difference in our lives. I've been very happy since thirteen. I was very glad to move to Guadalupe Carney where we have our own house, we all can go to school and study, Momi is closer to the hospital and medicines she needs, and Papi can work in the fields. I like studying hard. I know I can do a job that I want. I am studying to be a nurse. I am good at organizing things. And I am part of a craft co-op where I sell bracelets, earrings, and necklaces that I make from beads.

I actually love being in Guadalupe Carney because everything I need is there. I plan to get my nursing degree and return to work in our village. I worked my first year of practicum in the village health clinic. I took the exam and passed with the highest grades, therefore I could continue on to the good nursing program at the university in La Ceiba. (If you don't pass with high grades you can't go to La Ceiba, but need to go to another program that gives you a lesser degree in the end.) I rented a room outside of La Ceiba that also gave me food. But I had to pay so much for a taxi to school everyday that I didn't save any money doing this. I moved to a cheaper place that I share with three other students, but don't get any food. I take a bus to school daily. That is where I met a special man who worked as a runner for the bus company. He paid me a lot of attention everyday, and eventually asked me to meet him after work. We went to his apartment. He told me how special I

Norma volunteering at the clinic

Norma working at the craft store

was and how pretty I was (nobody had ever said this about me before.) He held me and kissed me. I knew my mother would be mad at me, but my body and mind didn't seem to be working together. That was the first time a man made love to me. I was torn in a million directions over my behavior. All week I worried about what I had done. The next week, he invited me to his apartment again…and I went, knowing and wanting. We made love again. This time, he told me how special and pretty I was and how much he loved me…and I was ready for more forever.

But a week later, I didn't get my period. I was mortified…and prayed this wasn't happening to me. I told him about this problem. He told me he didn't want kids, that I should have an abortion, or never see him again. I could never kill a baby…and certainly couldn't live with someone who would want me to do this. So now I am five months pregnant and alone. My parents were devastated at my indiscretion, but didn't disown me or anything. I talked to my teacher about continuing with classes,

which she has promised can be done, albeit not easily. I do have the highest grades in the class. If I quit to take care of my baby, I will have to reapply and start over in three years, since classes are already set with their quotas. I am determined to make this work, somehow. I won't give up my child, and I don't want to give up my nursing career that will give me a future job, and help me to help so many others in our village.

So I have traveled from the protective arms of my parents into the real world. It has been quite a lesson for me. I pray God will bless my decisions.

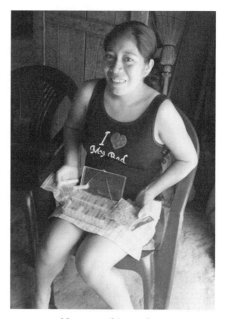

Norma working at home

Paula's Story

Bathing beauty

My Name is Maria Paula Lainez. I was born in Negrito, high in the mountains of Yoro, Honduras, on June 29th, 1970. I am the sixth of eight kids…four boys and four girls. When I was three we moved to San Antonio to work on a coffee finca that my father had bought. By the time I was eight, I was working the coffee fields with my brothers and sisters to get in the harvest. Our house had two rooms. Everyone slept in one room on three beds…three to a bed. Each bed was a wooden frame that was covered with a patate (woven mat).

My job was to carry water to the house. It was hard and heavy work. So when my mother bought a small pitcher just for me to carry this water, I purposely broke it on a rock, telling her it was an accident, of course. I really didn't like hauling water and thought this would be the way out of it. That didn't work since I then was given a real bucket just like everyone else.

My mother made me a rag doll from an old sock. Papi didn't like me playing with it, as is the custom with many Honduran fathers. Papi bought me a Molina to grind the family's corn for tortillas, and he made me a broom from grass so I could sweep the house…real woman's work. He had me working instead of playing. He taught me how to make rules. Momi taught me how to keep house and make tortillas. So that was my life as a child: cleaning the house, washing the clothes in the river, grinding corn for tortillas, and carrying water to the house. On special occasions we would get quajada, a homemade cheese. But usually we just ate rice and beans and tortillas everyday.

Once I remember wishing I could have new sandals…so I stretched out my old ones until they were useless. Then I had to get new ones. I was dreaming up ways to have a better life. I was conniving, but a dreamer.

By six years I was ready to go to school. It was far away. But it got even farther when three families began fighting over where to build the new school. My brothers and sisters and I had to go to the other school that was another two or three miles further away. Papi would only let me go to sixth grade, because he says a girl doesn't have much value, so doesn't need much education. He would buy us one pencil per year, shoes, and a uniform. He would make us a notebook at the beginning of each school year from folded paper and string, and gave us a cloth sack for a bookbag. In school I learned to read. It is something that I still love to do. My last year of school (sixth grade), my mother sold some eggs and chickens to buy me a beautiful light blue backpack. I loved that bag, and will never forget it.

Papi was very strict with all of us. He took us to the front row of the Catholic church twice a week. We couldn't turn our heads at all. If we looked around, he would grab our ears and wrench them to the front. I loved singing in church…and still love to lead the singing in our church in our village. We were not allowed to go to any celebrations at the church or at the school. Once my brothers and sisters and I snuck out to a church gathering. When Papi missed us he came and got us. We had asked permission from our mother. My older friend carried me on her shoulders. I got my earring caught in her hair, and we were giggling and trying to get untangled. Papi came at this moment and was very mad that we were clowning around and disobeying him. He took us all home and whipped us with a rod.

Paula is proud of buying a calf with her craft money

When I was twelve I got to go with my mother for a very special trip to visit my grandmother in Yoro. I was so excited. Momi bought me a beautiful light blue dress for the trip. There was a fair in Yoro at the time…something that I had never seen before. It was an amazing sight with all the excitement of the lights and people and colors and music. I laid awake all night dreaming of this fair and how I could tell my sisters about it.

Like so many mothers, my mother never told me about life and body changes. I was visitng my older sister in La Ceiba when I got my period for the first time. I had no idea what was going on, and was truly afraid. After a day of all this blood, thinking I was dying, I went to my sister, who explained things to me. She showed me how to use towels, and told me this would happen every month. This lesson taught me that I should explain things to my daughters so that they don't have to live through the fear that I did.

I knew Goyo from the village where we lived. He was handsome…and often drunk. He asked permission from Papi to talk with me. After a year of talking, we ran off to Goyo's brother's house in the mountains. I was seventeen. My parents were mad. This is the way things happen here in Honduras. But after eight days, Goyo went and talked to them, and they were OK. At nineteen, I had our first child, Judy. She now has my first grandchild, who was born just a month before Goyo was killed.

Yes, that was the saddest day of my life…the day Goyo died. I always knew he was a drinker and in danger from his drinking bouts. But after Judy was born, he began drinking more. I would run to my mother-in-law's to sleep, because I didn't know what Goyo was going to do when he was drunk. He was very unpredictable and could be violent. But when he was sober, he was a charmer, a good worker, and good husband. He cut wood for houses for a living. We had a nice wood house with a cement floor, electricity, and running water. We were raising four children in this house…until one day Goyo saw land in Guadalupe Carney with some others who were interested in getting land. This was two years before the group actually formed for the land takeover. We worked with the group for two years to get organized and ready for the move. The government had set this huge tract of land aside for land reform if any peasants wanted to claim it. Fifteen days before the invasion, Goyo went and built a house…. on an ant hill with no electric and no water. I was not sure this move was a good idea, but Goyo was positive it was the only way we were ever going to get any land of our own. So when the big truck came by, we piled our family on with our table, chair, and beds. We sold our TV and lights since there was no electric where we were headed.

But there was also no food! And no work. Nobody liked our group in the area so they wouldn't give anyone in our movement a job. We ate bananas with salt. Before this move, we had meals daily....now we had nothing. My cousin helped me open a small store in our house...but Goyo robbed the money for his liquor. I tried to do this for two years, but didn't get ahead. Then I went to a sewing class given by the government. There were ninety people in the class, but only ten of us got together as a sewing group. We had machines from the government for one and a half years. Then the government came and took them back and gave them to another group. We were expected to go to the sweat shops in San Pedro Sula or somewhere. That was why the class was offered for free, so the government could fulfill its commitment to the big factories. But our group didn't want to go away from our families. We asked a missionary to help us with ideas of things to make and sell. That was the beginning of a new life...a small zipper shoulder bag. We made enough money to buy machines of our own, and to give our husbands a loan to start a new cement block making business. They built us a sewing center with money donated for our project.

Goyo was happy. He had his land...we were still waiting for the titles that the government promised us. He had his cows...he was a good farmer and rancher. He had taken classes with a veterinarian who was working in our village. And he had a job with the blocks when he wasn't working on the land with the cows. Life was looking up. But he still got drunk too often. I would go hide in the sewing center with the kids when he went on a drunk. He would sometimes hit the kids or me. We never knew what he would do, so it was best to hide. We never told anyone where we were. Goyo never did know where our hiding place was.

The day Goyo was killed, he had been drinking. He made his way to Trujillo, and then needed to borrow a bike to get back because he missed the last bus. When he arrived, he went straight to the celebration in the center of our village. I was in the house asleep. Goyo and his friends were sitting at the paragua* and laughing at his close friend, Emilio, who was drunkenly showing off his new machete, swinging it up and down , and sideways. He accidentally slashed Goyo up his abdomen.

*paragua: a round, thatch-roofed building without any sides

Goyo tried to jump out of the way and defend himself with the borrowed bike…but too late. In his drunken stupor, he stumbled off and collapsed in the street while people came running to get me. We had to look for a car to get Goyo to the hospital…there were only three in the village. None had gas. So we then had to look for money to buy gas…and then find it. Once we got to the hospital in town, they told us they couldn't do anything and that we had to go to La Ceiba. Again, we had to look for money, gas, and car. The ride was terrible. Goyo was in and out of consciousness, crying in pain over every bump in the road… and there are many here in Honduras. We arrived in La Ceiba at the public hospital in the wee hours of the morning. They whisked Goyo into the surgery…and I never saw him again. He died after the surgery, they told me. They said he came thru the surgery fine and sent me off to the pharmacy to buy him some painkillers and antibiotics. When I returned, they told me Goyo was dead. He was my husband and friend. He was far from perfect, but we had a life together. I miss him. He helped me to teach our kids three important things: don't rob, respect others, and study hard. I have four wonderful children to remind me of my friend.

But life goes on. My name showed up on a list that an angry rancher put out for some people in our village to be killed. Since I was a village leader, my name was on the list. At first I just stayed home worrying about what to do. But I realized that this was no way to live…but I couldn't leave to work at the craft store or buy groceries…nothing. I also was worried

Crazy beach day

Paula sewing at the center

that my being here would jeopardize my children's safety. So one night, I left with Ericka, my third child. She had been having a hard time dealing with her father's death and was very nervous over me being on this list. She couldn't eat nor sleep. I took her to a hospital in La Ceiba, left her with my sister, and I went on to another country where I would be safe. My plan was to make it to the States for a job. But I don't have any papers and have no way of getting in there. So I am working as a housekeeper and getting paid well, sending money back to my children. Ericka returned to the village to live with her older sister. This didn't work out and she ran away to a brothel in Guatemala...I was so worried for her that I quit my job and went to get her. Together we have secretly returned to Honduras to take care of my aging father. My youngest daughter has moved from the village to live with us too. I will never be able to return to the village I worked so hard to help start. My oldest daughter has my one grandchild in the village. My son is living in our house in the village with his girlfriend. I pray for their safety and miss being a part of the life there.

Sewing group

Silvia's Story

Silvia cutting patterns

My name is Silvia Lainez Rodriguez. I was born in Negrito, Yoro in 1969. I am the fifth child of eight brothers and sisters, four boys, and four girls. We lived in a two room mud and thatch hut. Our beds were woven mats on the mud floor. Three of us shared a mat. My father worked for others, getting paid in beans. We ate only beans and tortillas, unless Papi caught some animal in the mountains. But I was chosen to leave the family when I was about five years old to go to live with my grandmother. She had nobody there to help her with the cleaning and washing. My mother had plenty of help and too many mouths to feed, so I was sent to Abuela. I led a charmed life with her, as she loved me deeply. Abuela gave me everything I needed. She bought me clothes, sent me to school, made sure I had good food, and lots of love from her. She taught me to have good values in my life. I felt very special.

Once in a while my older brothers would come to get me for a visit to my mother and the rest of the family. I loved this walk because they would put me on their shoulders and walk down the mountain. One time my brothers and sisters came for me. We were all walking back when we stumbled across a drunk guy laying in the path. He had a radio in the bushes beside him. We had never seen one of these things, and began playing with it. It seemed amazing to us that this box could make so many sounds. We decided to take it back to the house with us…even though we knew it was not ours. My brothers told me not to say anything about it. We hid it at the house for a couple days. Then the drunk guy came looking for it (he was no longer drunk). I was scared. My brothers gave it back, but our father was still mad at us for stealing. My brothers and sisters said it was my fault that they took it. They said I was crying and begging them to take it because I liked it so much. This wasn't true, of course, but because I was the special child, my brothers knew our parents wouldn't punish me and maybe not them if they said it was what I wanted to do.

75

At age twelve my father decided I had better move back home. I was beginning to mature and he was afraid I would run off with some guy and get pregnant. I was sad to leave my Abuela, but was happy to be with my family too. My mother taught me to cook because at my Grandmother's she did all the cooking for me. Sometimes I would go with my Papi to cut coffee in the finca. We lived in a cement house with a tin roof now, so life was a bit more comfortable than the mud floor house.

I had many boyfriends in my teenage years. But Raul won my heart when I was fifteen. He was handsome and could sing and play guitar. I loved singing, so this was a wonderful guy to have around. One night when my Papi had gone to Jutiyalpa, Raul and I ran off to Tela, a town on the north coast of Honduras. We stayed there one month before we returned to his parents' house. For the next two years, I stayed at home, and Raul worked in a rice co-op. On a small part of his parents' land, he built us a house of cement blocks and wood with a tin roof and eventually electricity. After two years, I was pregnant with our first child. We had a total of six children, three boys and three girls. After the first three, we got married in the church. This was important to us because we wanted to participate in the church services and couldn't do this if we were not married. Raul loved to play his guitar and I loved to lead the singing. The Catholic church is very strict about your relations outside of the marriage. We had a small wedding for just us and our family members.

In 1998 Hurricane Mitch ravaged Honduras. We lost our house and our jobs…no rice for the co-op. We had no way of getting work and now had a large family to feed. Everyone was in the same situation, so things were not looking to get better. We heard about a meeting of people who were going to take over a piece of land near Trujillo. It was land that the Honduras government put aside for the poor people to live on if they wanted to. We were part of the original planning of this group that grew to over 10,000 people. It was a two year plan that helped us to get organized before we actually moved to the land. We were divided into groups of about fifteen families per group, to help us communicate our concerns better and watch out for one another. We had to give money, time and work to the group. A date was set for the move.

When that day came, we were filled with excitement and fear. We would be getting a large piece of land that would be OURS…but we were leaving the security of family and the house we knew. Raul had gone the week before to put up a small temporary house for us, so that we could arrive without having to build a house quickly. It was made of cane and thatch with a mud floor. He had heard some people didn't want us to move to this land and may cause us problems. But we didn't truly believe this would happen. A large truck that usually hauls oranges came to pick us up. There were about five other families in the truck with all their possessions. We took two beds, our cups and dishes, and our clothes. It was all we had left after the hurricane. Raul and I joined this movement in hopes of having a better future for our children and living on a larger lot than we had in our old house. This move was for the possibility of having a piece of land for us and our family.

We arrived in mass confusion...even though we tried to organize things before we began the move. People went to their plots and began putting up their houses of mud and sticks. Some just slept under the stars. All of us suffered on that first night...ants. Yes, this entire piece of land was a giant ant farm. We were all eaten alive by morning. It was terrible. The house Raul built was very small, not comfortable, and filled with ants. All I wanted to do was leave....but I had no money for bus fare back. I held my babies so they wouldn't get bit...and tried to find a place to stand where I could guard us and cry. We had no place to go, so, like everyone else, we stayed and helped the group to claim the land. Many land owners from Trujillo met us on our arrival with guns and pistols. They were not happy about our arrival in their municipality. They thought we would put strain on their already fragile health and education systems. Some people in our group got killed...that stirred things up...but also made the rich folks back off. They fought us for the next ten years on and off. There were many court battles, but we are slowly but surely getting our titles to the land that was set aside for us.

I took a sewing course that was offered to women in the group. Ten of us decided to start a sewing co-op. We made curtains and altered used clothing for villagers. Nobody had money to pay us, so we

Silvia and Raul

Silvia showing the craft products

didn't make anything. We were using treadle machines that the government loaned to us for two years. At the end of two years they would come to get the machines back, and hopefully we would all go to a sweat shop to work. Or that was the government's plan. But none of us wanted to leave the village and our families. So we looked for a woman we heard helped folks with ideas of things to make. Diane came to meet us and loved our work. She helped us find some ideas that tourists would buy, therefore we could charge money that would actually give us an income. Our first product was a small zippered bag on a shoulder strap. I remember watching the tourists buying them and being amazed at how they liked our products so much. We have developed many other bags over the years. And now we are painting silk scarves. I love my work.

In August, 2008, there was a terrible fire at the house on the property that our group was taking over. This man would not give up his house nor his land, even though he had no title. The government told him to move, but he wouldn't. So daily we would go and sit on the land to claim it as ours. For years he had been sending people to shoot the villagers who were watching the land. So we decided to send a group instead of just the one or two that had been going. This man sent five armed guards with AK-47's and dressed in riot gear at 5:00 AM to kill our group. The group scattered, but not before one villager was killed and another wounded. We called the police for help, but they couldn't do anything because this man was a police commissioner and ruled with a heavy hand. So villagers went to his house and surrounded it, demanding that the five armed guards come out. Of course they didn't! Eventually, somebody in the crowd set fire to the house, killing everyone inside, nine people. This was a grave mistake that caused more problems. The man was more than angry. He made a list of village leaders and people he thought might have been at the house. He wanted them arrested and killed. Raul was on that list…even though he was nowhere near the burning house. But

Silvia with her grandkids

this meant he could not leave the village safely for any work because buses were being stopped and searched for villagers. The entire village was being held hostage. As money ran out, food became scarce. Raul decided to leave with some other guys in the village to get work in Nicaragua. This was a tough decision, but one he felt he had to make since we could see no answer by staying in the house. Raul was gone for almost a year. It was difficult for us, since food and money just weren't there. But when he came back, he did have some cash…and not long after that, the arrest list was taken away. And not long after that, the government came and gave us titles to the land.

So you see, life is like a mountain…up high and down low and up and down. I am guessing this is the way it goes on to eternity. Last year we got electricity at our house. I still love singing at church. I love my sewing. I have my children and grandchildren living with me. And I have my Raul back. Can life get any better?

Silvia and Raul with their kids and grandkids

Tonia's Story

Tonia wearing her coconut shell jewelry

My name is Maria Antonia Paz Roble. People call me Tonia. I am from Morazon, Yoro. I think I am thirty-three years old, but am never sure because I don't know what year I was born...nor what day is my birthday. Since we never celebrated birthdays in our family, it was something my mother forgot...if she ever knew. Elias has always told me I am one year younger than he is, so since he was born in 1971, that means I was born in 1972. But I don't really know if he knows this or has made it up. I do know we have been together for many years...at least five years as boyfriend and girlfriend before I moved in with him. We knew each other many years before that since we lived in the same village all our lives, and his house was only feet away from our family's house. We have two teenage daughters.

In Morazon, we all lived in mud houses with thatched roofs, no plumbing or electricity. My family slept on bed frames strung with cord and put patates on top...but I didn't sleep well there, so they let me have the hammock. The whole family had to carry water for over a mile each way for drinking. We washed our clothes and dishes and bathed in that same small stream. Work was expected of all of us, except the baby...she never had to do anything.

I was the fifth of six kids. I remember playing with my three older brothers and sister, making mud tortillas and cakes. We'd feed each other our special dinners. We also liked to make up dances and perform for each other. We had no music, but that didn't matter. And we had our own church services, taking turns being the preacher. We spent our days occupying each other while our father was hunting in the mountains. He often took my brothers with him. Our mother stayed in the house all the time, cooking, and cleaning. It was my job to make the family's tortillas daily...a big stack. When our mother got mad at us for something, she got

Family Christmas picture

really mad, screaming and yelling at us to get things done.

When my last sister was born, I got the job of caring for her. It was fun since I never had any baby doll to play with, and she was like a doll. I was ten years old when she was born, and took care of her every need until I left the house eight years later.

My father was a nice man. He would take us with him to cut coffee, harvest beans, or make compost. We liked these excursions to the mountains. He worked hard to keep us fed. The saddest day of my life was the day he died. He had been suffering with prostate problems for some time. His death was terrible to watch as he couldn't breathe. I remember him fondly.

Every Sunday our family would go to the Catholic church near us. It was just expected that we go. Since I have moved here to Trujillo, I don't go to the Catholic church, but attend a protestant church that is near our house. The Catholic church is too far away for us to walk to regularly. But worshipping God is important and it doesn't matter what church you attend to do this.

Holidays were great in our village. I remember the 'correo de cinta' on the 15th of September, our Independence Day. This is a race where the guys ride a horse and have a pencil in their hand. They try to put the pencil thru a ring that is hanging on a string as they pass by. If they won, they got a handkerchief that was pinned to the shoulder of the dress of the girls in the

Tonia with her nativity figures

Trying new ideas

crowd. They also got a kiss. It was fun to watch and be part of the crowd.

Christmas was also a big day. Here in Honduras, we celebrate the 24th of

Family working together

December with tamales and bread. Friends and family from other parts come and share with us. We loved having all the company, and new kids to play with. To this day, I like holidays because our entire family gets together to celebrate.

My brother had moved to Trujillo and said there was work to be had there. After Mitch, things in Yoro were bad, and there was no work. So we decided to move to Trujillo and see what we could find. We lived with my brother until Elias got a job. We are the watchmen on a beach property, caring for the house and keeping the yard cut and flowers blooming. Elias also makes cement blocks. But the job we like the most is making necklaces, earrings, and nativities from coconut shells. I am part of a co-op that has a small store near Trujillo where we sell our crafts. It is fun to see people buying things you know you have made with your own hands.

I started out making mirrors lined with shells and sea glass. They were pretty ways to decorate your house with reminders of the beach. A gringa friend, Diane, showed me how to make these mirrors. She also showed us the other ideas that we make. The coconut shell necklaces and earrings, and the nativities made of fimo* and coconut shell mangers. This gringa taught us the importance of doing things right so that people will appreciate the quality of our work.

Someday I hope to have enough money saved to build a nice house. We live in the watchman's building now...and it belongs to the owners of the property. I hope we can someday have our own place, but we seem to spend all the money we make. We have a small piece of land to build on someday. My other hopes are for my girls to be married and to know how to take care of their houses and families well.

Tonia, Elias, Rosa and Desi

*fimo: plastic modeling clay

Ubaldo's Story

Ubaldo showing his work

I am Jose Ubaldo Suarez, but am called Ubaldo by friends and family. I was born in El Obrja, an aldea* just outside Choluteca, in Honduras on May 16th, 1963. I am the youngest of thirteen kids, in a Catholic family that sometimes went to church. We lived in a large mud hut house with a tile roof. All of us had jobs to do around the house. The girls helped my mother with the housework, the guys helped my father to plant the corn or to clean the corn. Then we would put half of it in the big wooden box for use by our family. We would sell the other half to the market vendors in Choluteca.

Our family was very poor, but usually had food. Unlike most people think, rice was not part of our daily diet. It was not grown nearby and was too expensive to have often. We did, however, have beans and quajada (homemade cheese), and often chicken from our yard.

I went to school thru sixth grade. Since we were a very poor family, as were the other families in our area, we didn't have to buy uniforms. This made it possible for me to go to school. I never had a pair of shoes on my feet until I was seventeen years old, but that didn't stop me from playing my favorite sport, soccer. At school I was a good student. I loved math, and writing Gothic letters. At recess my friends and I would often play marbles, using seeds from a tree for the marbles and a seed from another tree for the shooter.

I got my first job outside the house with my brother at a chair caning factory in our town. The factory got vines from Japan that we would weave into patterns on chair parts. We only had this job for a year because a labor union came in and said they had to pay more to each

*aldea: village

person, and they couldn't hire kids to work there. This closed them down.

I got a really bad kidney infection where my stomach was bloated and I turned yellow. I was unconscious for three days in the hospital. They thought I would die. I remember waking up and feeling a nurse poking me with a pin all over my body. It got my attention and I woke up. They sent me home to recuperate for there for the next five months.

I still loved playing soccer and was a very competitive player. I got in a fight with another player during a game. He was so mad at me that he later chased me down with a knife, stabbing me four times. I ran to my parents' house, where they decided I had to get out of town. They put me on a bus to Colon where my older brother lived. That arrangement only lasted a year because it was difficult living with my brother and his family.

I went back to Choluteca to help my father in the campo*. That is when I saw a girl I thought I'd like to know better. Since she went to the Seventh Day Adventist church, I decided to go there too. While attending this church to see this girl, I accepted Christ into my life. The girl left with another guy, but Christ is still part of my life in a big way, since I now co-pastor a different church with my brother.

At twenty-four years old, I was walking to church with my brother, when soldiers came and kidnapped me off the road. My brother saw this,

Ubaldo with his daughter and pictures

*campo: countryside

but couldn't do anything. My parents didn't know where they took me for months. This was the way of recruitment here in Honduras in those days. This was during the time of the Contra-Sandinista conflict, so I was taken to the battalion to learn how to fight the Sandinistas in case they came into Honduras. I was in the battalion for only eight months and guarded the Honduras/ Nicaragua border for only four days. But these eight months were the worst days of my life. Ten soldiers in our group didn't like me because I am a Christian. They would torture me in whatever way they could. They pushed me down, banged my head, and loved slamming my fingertips with a paddle. Daily I preached God's word to the group, and most were appreciative, but afraid to do anything when these guys began their beatings with me. One day I decided I had to get out of there or I would die. I went to my commander and told him I needed to leave and go preach. Five days later, he called me into his office and handed me my exit card, which I carry with me all the time to prove I have done my time in the military.

I left as rapidly as possible and went straight back to my parents' house. By this time, both of my parents were no longer Catholic, but attending another evangelical church. I went with them and met Rosalia. I had known her before this, since she was living in our same aldea. For one year and three months I went to her house and sat and talked with her and her parents, to show them I was honorable and had good intentions for their daughter. I was working in the campo with my father during the days and courting in the evenings.

Rosalia and I got married in the church. It was a simple service with friends and family. We had a celebration with a pig roast, tamales, and cakes. I became the pastor of a small church that had a house attached, where we went to live. Our job was to work with the unwed couples in the church, to bring them to Christ. This is when our first daughter was born.

At this point our church decided to send me to Orlancho, a state in Honduras known for its outlaw justice. I thought it was too dangerous for my wife and child, so refused to go. They fired me.

Again I returned to my parents' home in Choluteca. We lived there five years, during which time our second daughter was born. We helped my parents with the family work. Then we left for Trujillo, where my brother had built a non-denominational church. I was thirty years old with nothing. I built a mud house on the bit of land (about fifteen feet square) that we still live on today. The house fills the whole lot. During this time I began painting, something I had never done before. I would see pictures in old discarded magazines or on posters, and would go home and try to reproduce them in my watercolors and notebook. A few years later Hurricane Mitch pounded our walls into mud and blew our house down. It nearly fell on us as we just got out before it fell. We could save nothing. It was devastating to our family. They didn't like me painting because it didn't bring in any steady income for the house. My brother taught me how to be a foreman in construction, of which there were many jobs after Mitch. With money from this job, I bought an art book that taught me how to look at distance and perspective, colors, and more. I poured over this book to learn as much as I could. But I could only paint in my spare time since it was not bringing in much money. When I wasn't working construction, I was walking the streets of Tocoa and Trujillo trying to sell my paintings.

That is how I met Maria. She and her partner were part of a group of artists who were starting a co-op to sell their goods. She invited me to come and sell with them. Being part of a group is hard for me since I am used to doing things on my own. But after I learned to take the criticism

Ubaldo's family 'car'

constructively, I began selling more. The group helps each other with new ideas and to identify good products. I am now the secretary of the co-op, Made In Honduras. We sell mainly to workteams that pass through the area. I paint pictures of all sizes, magnets, and make wooden boxes and boats. We all have to work at the store two days per month to keep the store open. We meet monthly to review the needs of the co-op. I am pleased with my work and with this opportunity I have to sell it.

In all of my years, my most precious moments are when God has spoken to me. It is usually in a song at church, but it is also in memories of my marriage to a wonderful woman, the births of my two daughters and two sons, and in celebrations in our family. I give God thanks for everything He has given me.

Ubaldo with Rosalia and children